UNITY LIBRARY 8 ARCHIVES
All shall be well : the spiritu
BX 2350 .L56 1982

0 0051 0032777 7

ALL SHALL BE WELL

D0170254

The Lord looks upon his servant
with pity and not with blame
(Julian of Norwich, *Revelations of Divine Love*,
chapter 82)

ALL SHALL BE WELL

The Spirituality of Julian of Norwich
for Today

ROBERT LLEWELYN

UNITY SCHOOL LIBRARY
UNITY VILLAGE, MISSOURI 64065

Paulist Press
New York/Mahwah

6/01

All royalties earned by the sale of this book are being given to The Julian Shrine, c/o All Hallows, Rouen Road, Norwich (England).

First published 1982 as *With Pity Not Blame*
by Darton, Longman & Todd Ltd, London

Copyright © 1982 by
Robert Llewelyn

All rights reserved. No part of this book may be reproduced or transmitted in any form or by any means, electronic or mechanical, including photocopying, recording, or by any information storage and retrieval system without permission in writing from the publisher.

Library of Congress
Catalog Card Number: 84-62985

ISBN:0-8091-2668-0

Published by Paulist Press
997 Macarthur Boulevard
Mahwah, N.J. 07430

Printed and bound in the United States of America

gift

Contents

BX
2350
.L56
1982
c. 1

Preface

This book is based on *The Revelations of Divine Love* of Julian of Norwich and explores her way of prayer and some of the fundamental aspects of her writings. The mode of some chapters is exposition and interpretation, of others reflection upon some particular insight and its development. My own understanding and application of Julian will be evident throughout. In some of the later chapters I have briefly explored the way of contemplative prayer based on the Dionysian tradition and developed in *The Cloud of Unknowing*. Julian could almost certainly not have read *The Cloud* before writing her *Revelations*, though later she might perhaps have done so. We may, however, assume that her way of contemplative prayer would have been similar, and some examination of the teaching of *The Cloud* will supplement Julian's own written insights on prayer.

The book owes its origin to retreat addresses over the past five years, mostly to religious communities, but to clergy, parishes and students as well. The addresses have, however, been considerably expanded and extensively rewritten. At the same time I have thought it best to leave a certain informality as a reminder of the note of personal encounter which is basic to the approach of a retreat. It is hoped that with the growing number who are today coming under the spell of Julian's writings, the book will have an appeal at a general level.

Robert Llewelyn
The Julian Shrine, c/o All Hallows, Rouen Road, Norwich

Acknowledgements

Thanks are due to the following for permission to reproduce extracts from copyright sources.

Paulist Press: *Julian of Norwich: Showings*, eds. Edmund Colledge, OSA and James Walsh, SJ, 1979.

Penguin Books Ltd: *Revelations of Divine Love* by Julian of Norwich, tr. Clifton Wolters (Penguin Classics 1966). Copyright © Clifton Wolters 1966. *The Cloud of Unknowing and Other Works*, tr. Clifton Wolters (Penguin Classics, Revised edition, 1978). Copyright © Clifton Wolters 1961, 1978. Reprinted by permission of Penguin Books Ltd.

SLG Press, Fairacres, Oxford: *Prayer and Contemplation* and *The Positive Role of Distraction in Prayer*, both by Robert Llewelyn.

Abbreviations

LT, EC and JW ST, EC and JW	Edmund Colledge, OSA, and James Walsh, SJ, *Julian of Norwich: Showings*. SPCK 1979. The book contains the Longer Text (LT) and the Shorter Text (ST).
LT, CW	Clifton Wolters, *Julian of Norwich, Revelations of Divine Love*. Penguin Classics 1973. The book contains the Longer Text only.
E in L	*Enfolded in Love: Daily Readings with Julian of Norwich*. Darton, Longman and Todd 1980.
CU, CW PC, CW	Clifton Wolters, *The Cloud of Unknowing and Other Works*. Penguin Classics. CU = *The Cloud of Unknowing*, PC = *The Epistle of Privy Counsel*. Both are contained in the one book. 1978. In cases in which quotations from the same chapter run consecutively an indicator number is shown against one of them only.

1

Julian and Her Cell Today

In the early summer of 1974, a blind man, assisted by his companion and driven by some strange compulsion, made his way to Norwich to visit the Julian Cell. Many years before he had been a prisoner of war in the hands of the Japanese. He had been severely treated and his present blindness was one of the scars carried from those days. As he and his friend knelt together in the silence of the cell he became aware of the reason for his strange journey. Julian herself appeared and with her she brought the Japanese soldier responsible for his suffering. The dead man had come to seek the forgiveness of his war-time victim, who himself had not been able to overcome the bitterness felt against his captor. What then took place none can tell, only that the blind man was heard to speak to his visitor in Japanese; and, released from his resentment in the reconciliation which followed, he lapsed into an ecstasy of joy. The two made their way to All Hallows convent guest-house next door, where they were given tea by one of the Sisters. During tea in her presence the vision was repeated, and the blind man poured out his heart in great animation once more in Japanese. The vision was for him only, and not for his companions who saw nothing; though in any case the fact of his blindness indicates that we are not speaking of the ordinary channels of seeing. Understanding now the reason for his journey and knowing that reconciliation had been effected, the blind man left in great happiness. He has since died, and I have felt free to tell his experience.

Whatever the reader may make of this story, it portrays Julian in the rôle she exercised for many years—and exercises anew today—of mediating the love of God to those burdened by their sins, and in the power of that love bringing reconciliation and peace to men of good will. Who is this Julian, so little known that probably not one person in a hundred in her native city could find their way to her cell, yet so well known that pilgrims visit the site from all over the world, and men like T. S. Eliot and Thomas Merton herald her as one of the most wonderful of all Christian voices?[1] One who has made a study of the English mystics of the fourteenth century—Richard Rolle, Walter Hilton, the unknown author of *The Cloud of Unknowing*—coming finally to Mother Julian writes:

> Historical comparisons are seldom fair and often absurd; but when we see the sparkle and taste the flavour of the Lady Julian's vintage we are tempted to affirm that the best wine has been kept until last. Not a few would go further; some of the Saint's admirers are prepared to assert that in all the shining ranks of mystics, in this and other lands, none can dim the brightness of this ancress of Norwich. Those who have fallen beneath the spell of this gracious lady, and whose interior life has been quickened by the power and beauty of her *Revelations,* will readily pardon this flicker of insular pride.[2]

*

We must own at once that we know very little about Julian. There is, however, as we shall see, one important date which fastens her into history—8 May 1373—and as she tells us that she was then thirty and a half years old, we may give 1342 with some certainty as the date of her birth. She is mentioned in several wills and from them we learn she had two servants, Sara and Alice, in her later years. The latest bequest—of twenty shillings to Julian 'recluz' at Norwich—is in 1416, though it is possible that a will of 1423 also refers to Julian. A little earlier the scribe editor who introduces the Shorter Text of Julian's 'shewings' speaks of her as 'a devout woman whose name is Julian. . . a recluse at Norwich . . . living yet in this year of our Lord 1413'. The historian Blomefield writing in 1768 makes reference to her anchorage, which stood until the 'Dissolution, when the house was demolished', and speaks of Julian as one 'esteemed of the greatest holiness'.[3] The date of her death is not known, but we cannot be far wrong in surmising that she lived to about eighty years, which would have been a good old age in those days. Her grave is without trace. Nor do we know anything of her parentage and birth—not even her name, for it is generally assumed that she took the name Julian from the little church to which her cell was attached, which was then some four hundred years old.[4]

For many years there had been no knowledge of any contemporary reference to Julian other than those cited above. Then in 1936 there came the exciting discovery of *The Book of Margery Kempe,* known to exist but lost to history for five centuries. Margery was a prominent citizen of King's Lynn, about forty miles from Norwich, and she graphically relates a visit to 'Dame Jelyan', on whose spiritual discernment and good counsel she knew she could rely. The date is uncertain but would probably have been early in the second decade of the new century. Julian would have been about seventy, and her *Revelations of Divine Love* would have been written some twenty years before. Margery's description of the counsel she received bears fascinating resemblance to what we know of Julian from her own writings. The visit was evidently a great success: 'Much was the holy dalliance that the anchoress and this creature had by communing in the love of our Lord Jesus Christ on the many days they were together.'[5]

Julian is known to us today for a series of sixteen 'shewings' given to her on 8 May 1373, centred on the Holy Trinity and the person and passion of Jesus. It seems that she first wrote them down within a short time of receiving them, adding such commentary as her own meditations suggested. After that there is silence for about twenty years, when she wrote the book for which she is now remembered, *The Revelations of Divine Love,* known and treasured throughout the Christian world. In many respects it follows closely the Shorter Text written twenty years before, but it is necessarily more mature and much enlarged, being about four times the length of the earlier book. It is a work marked by the depth of its theology, the breadth of its compassion and the almost unrivalled beauty of its language. We shall draw out some of its teaching in the chapters which follow, in some cases quoting extensively from its pages. It will be referred to as the Longer Text, distinguishing it from the Shorter Text of twenty years before.[6]

Julian relates the circumstances of her 'shewings' in both texts, which should, if possible, be taken together at this point. 8 May 1373 fell on the third Sunday after Easter, and Julian had been lying desperately ill for a week. Neither she nor those around her thought she would survive, and three days before, her parish priest had already given her the last rites. 'I was quite convinced that I was passing away—as indeed were those about me.'[7] But although she was a young woman of but thirty years, and anxious to live if she might thereby serve God better, the prospect of death held no fears; indeed she recalled how once she had prayed for just such a sickness—if it were in accordance with God's will—hoping she might thus be profitably tested. Now that it was upon her she accepted it in an act of full and generous surrender, praying, 'Good Lord, let my ceasing to live be to your glory!' 'Reason and suffering alike', she tells us, 'told me I was going to die, so I surrendered my will wholeheartedly to the will of God.'[8] Once again, this time in the very early hours of Sunday morning, her priest was summoned that he might be with her at her passing. He came bringing with him a small boy bearing a crucifix, but by this time her eyes were fixed and she could not speak. Holding the crucifix before her he bade her look upon it, saying, 'I have brought you the image of your Maker and Saviour. Look at it and be strengthened.' Even as she was seemingly sinking into death, her body without feeling from the upper part downwards, her life was remarkably restored. 'Suddenly all my pain was taken away, and I was as fit and well as I had ever been.'[9] It was then about four o'clock as dawn was breaking that her revelations were given her, fifteen between now and perhaps three in the afternoon ('none of the day') and one on the following night, these too coming as a gift she had prayed for, provided always it might be God's will she should receive it.

Julian mentions that her mother was among those present at her bedside and tells how she inadvertently caused distress by a gesture:

My mother, who was standing there with the others, held up her hand in front of my face to close my eyes, for she thought that I was already dead or had that moment died; and this greatly increased my sorrow, for despite all my pains, I did not want to be hindered from seeing (Christ), because of my love for him.[10]

The passage is interesting since it is one of several indications that Julian was conscious and awake at the time of her 'shewings'; it may also indicate the part played by the crucifix held before her eyes in supplying the setting for what she saw. In spite of the darkness, which she tells us was around her, 'there was ordinary light trained upon the image of the cross, I did not know how'.[11]

We can hardly be wrong in thinking that it was at some time after her 'shewings' that Julian embraced the solitary life. The presence of her mother and friends at her bedside is alone sufficient to indicate that that was so. It was a vocation not uncommon in those days, and half a century before Julian's time fifty or more solitaries are known to have been attached to churches or other buildings in Norwich alone. We also know the names of five anchoresses who occupied Julian's own cell successively up to well into the sixteenth century. The vocation may seem strange to our contemporary society with its relish for 'useful' activities, but Julian belonged to a world which, however far it might fall below the ideals it cherished, regarded a life dedicated to prayer and contemplation as the most important of all callings. Canon A. M. Allchin writes:

> She was a citizen of a city which put at its centre a cathedral, not because it was thought that it would make a beautiful addition or adornment to a society which had already been constructed, but because men believed that worship and prayer were the most vital and necessary of all human activities.[12]

But the solitary did too perform a useful function in the more general understanding of those words. Each cell had a window which looked on to the 'world' and the anchorite— or the anchoress as the case might be—would have fulfilled in part a number of offices today distributed among people as varied as social workers, marriage counsellors, Samaritans, psychiatrists, clergy and others. Fridays were to be kept in complete silence, and a few other days depending on the church season, but otherwise, though with plentiful warnings against abuse and over-indulgence, the anchoress might use her discretion in talking with visitors. Her knowledge, it is true, might often be rudimentary, but an attentive ear and an understanding heart, supported by a few simple and loving words, or scriptural teaching, spoken in the wisdom of the Holy Spirit, may be assumed to have had power to penetrate the secret recesses of the heart more surely than would the sophisticated advice of worldly people.

Julian's natural and spontaneous delight in God as her father and mother suggests a serene and happy childhood. Perhaps she came from a home of some substance, her description of Jesus as a kindly nurse[13] with no other care but for the welfare of his children finding its origin in the memory of some beloved nurse of childhood days. It has often been supposed that she received her education from the Sisters of the Benedictine convent at Carrow, within a mile of her later anchorage. Perhaps later she herself took the habit and experienced her 'shewings' as a Benedictine nun. That supposition would fit in with the internal evidence of the book which suggests a woman of some education. Thomas Merton calls her 'a true theologian' who 'really elaborates theologically the content of her revelations'.[14] Julian's own reference to herself as 'unlettered'[15] may be taken to mean no more than that she had little or no working knowledge of Latin. Her book is the first known book to be written by a woman in English.

Here we have been largely in the area of guesswork. We are on firmer ground when we speak of Julian's background on the broader canvas of history. Her early years were lived through what may well have been the most traumatic period England has ever known. The Black Death, a form of bubonic plague, struck when Julian was six years old and cut off perhaps a third of the population of the land. Norwich suffered as badly as any city, one estimate saying that less than a half of its population survived. When Julian was eighteen the plague struck again, and there was a third outbreak, though milder, when she was twenty-seven. The cries of the dying, the loneliness and suffering and grief of little children, the smell of decaying flesh in the streets, the burials in mass graves, the horror of rats and vermin would all have been familiar to her. They must surely have left their mark on the life and writing of one as sensitive as Julian.

*

The site of Julian's cell today is still marked by two fragments of stone jutting out from the walls of the church, dating back to Julian's time or before. These have been incorporated into the present cell, which is now furnished as a chapel and is rather more than twice the size of the estimated hundred square feet of the original. It was built and consecrated shortly after the Second World War, in which the church had been badly damaged by enemy action. On most days the Eucharist is celebrated and the many and varied intercessory requests are regularly offered. Also extending from the church a small library and counselling-room have been created to meet the growing pastoral needs. Both look on to a garden to the south of the church, where visitors may sit or walk or eat their picnic meals. Immediately next door is All Hallows, a convent guest-house run by two Sisters of the Community of All Hallows who care for those who wish to make a longer stay. The whole stands for a place of pilgrimage and prayer, and too as a symbol of unity, for Julian's wisdom and sanity transcend all denominational boundaries.

In her cell on this spot Julian of Norwich lived and prayed, took her meals and slept, worked at some simple task such as needlework, meditated on her book and wrote its pages, and counselled many from her little window looking on to the street, which in her day ran where the garden now stands. Opposite there was another window through which she could see into the church, hear mass and receive communion. It is thus that she spent twenty, thirty, perhaps forty years. As we have said, we can give no certain date to her death; nor do we know at what period she received her call to the solitary life. Julian's life has passed largely into obscurity, and no doubt this is how she would have wished it. 'You shall soon forget me', she writes, '(and do so that I shall not hinder you) and behold Jesus who is teacher of all.'[16]

2

Humility True and False

Bishop Edward Wynn of Ely—of beloved memory—used to tell the story of a young man who asked an elderly priest if he could recommend a good book on humility. The older man reflected for a few moments and then replied quite simply that the best book he knew on humility was a little book he had written himself. It was only a truly humble man, the Bishop would say, who would speak like that. After all, as St Teresa has told us, humility *is* truth.

Humility is a suspect virtue in many quarters and understandably so, for there is a false note in much which passes under its name. Julian is not blind to the spurious humility by which we may easily deceive ourselves and inhibit the working of God's grace. In one of the most important single sentences of her book, addressed as always to her 'even-Christians' and referred to here as God's lovers, she says that in her opinion what hinders spiritual growth more than any other single thing is the failure on our part to believe that God will most surely bring to completion the work he has begun. We shall in a moment see how this attitude links with false humility, but let us first follow Julian's thought.

> Some of us believe that God is all powerful and may do everything; and that he is all wise and can do everything; but as for believing that he is all love and will do everything, there we hold back. In my view nothing hinders God's lovers more than the failure to understand this.[1]

Julian then traces in what is surely an autobiographical note the sequence through which we pass. As we grow to hate our past sins and reach out towards amendment of life we are hindered by a nagging fear. Can God really forgive the sins of the past? And even if he can, then what about the present, with our resolutions to do better? Almost before we have begun we are down once more. And where does this doubting fear inevitably lead? Says Julian, it 'makes us so woebegone and so depressed that we can scarcely see any consolation'.[2] Yet none of this would be too bad (is the implication) if we recognized it as bad. But—and here comes the thrust—'sometimes we take this fear for humility'.[3] It is not so, says Julian, and writing in no uncertain terms she says that far from being an expression of humility this anxiety is 'a reprehensible blindness and weakness . . . and, (echoing Teresa) 'is contrary to truth'. All this comes about simply because we have forgotten the love in which we are held—its faithfulness and our need to rejoice in it—or (referring back) we have failed to take to ourselves the most basic of all truths that because God is all love he will see to it—must see to it—that the work he has begun will not be left unfinished. And so to the final words of the chapter: 'As by his courtesy God forgives our sins when we repent, even so he wills that we should forgive our sins; and so give up our senseless worrying and faithless fear.'[4]

A further form of false humility is to be found in the depreciation of our qualities or capacities in which we sometimes indulge. Julian does not mention this, perhaps because in contrast with the other it is relatively harmless. We do not deceive ourselves, and if we are speaking to people who know us well—for whom we usually keep such remarks!—we probably do not deceive them either. Our words are most likely prompted by a need for reassurance and encouragement; and we cannot, after all, expect to be told that we are generous and loving until we have first volunteered that we are mean and uncaring. It is little more than a lover's game, and it may be seen as part of the courtesy of love to play along with it. Yet if we were truly humble we would not feel the need to speak in this way, but would rather be happily content in the work God has well in hand and uninterested in gauging our spiritual pulse.

Or again, we betray ourselves into a false humility when we say—one example must stand for all—that we hope to take a second class in our examination when we are fully expecting a first. In such instances we are acting in self-defence, opening up a way of escape lest the papers do not suit us and our vanity is pricked. It exposes our fear of being humbled and to that extent our pride is revealed. But here, too, we hardly deceive ourselves, and our face-saving device is probably apparent to others as well.

Scarcely deceiving even ourselves, the above pretences are comparatively innocuous. It is, as always, the lie which we mistake for the truth which heralds disaster, and it is this with which Julian deals. Let us make no mistake, and Julian here speaks with great urgency, that we are on a disaster course, hell bent (albeit unwittingly) on our own destruction and spreading negative emotions all around us, when we settle with ourselves that our past sins or present weaknesses have somehow put us beyond the range of God's mercy. Yet to say that, and to leave it there, is still to miss the full thrust of Julian's point; which is that just because we mistake our state for humility, which is necessarily pleasing to God, we remain content with it and so deprive ourselves of any motivation to claim and trust and rejoice in the limitless generosity of God's love. Believing ourselves to be moving into life, we are sinking into death. Julian's words are to set us free to rise to the acceptance of the peace and joy and forgiveness which already await us.

Turning now from the humility which is false to that which is true, we shall find that for Julian it is to be found as an offshoot of the contemplation of God. It is a grace which steals in unnoticed as we turn our attention from it. It is a by-product of worship. Yet here at once we meet with a difficulty. We are to worship God, so far as that is possible for fallen people, for his sake and not for what we may get from him. The more our eyes are on the fruits of worship, the less plentiful (or we may say the more tarnished) will those fruits in fact be. Paralleling the Everest climbers we are, so far as it is given us, to worship God because he is there.

Julian gives expression to this thought in chapter 10 of the Longer Text, where she writes that the contemplation of God is not only the greatest honour to him, but the greatest profit to the soul, and it is in this activity that 'it receives most humility and other virtues',[5] and she adds: 'For it seems to

✗ me that the greatest honour which a soul can pay to God is simply to surrender itself to him with true confidence whether it be seeking or contemplating.' She returns to this thought later on, writing that the contemplation of God 'makes the creature marvellously meek and mild'.[6] But it is in chapter 7 that we find Julian's classic reference to humility, taking its place in the text almost incidentally in her moving description of her vision of 'our Lady, Saint Mary'. The passage deserves to be quoted in full:

> Our Lord showed me our Lady, Saint Mary, to teach us this: that it was the wisdom and truth in her, when she beheld her maker, that enabled her to know him as so great, so holy, so mighty and so good. His greatness and his nobleness overwhelmed her. She saw herself so little and low, so simple and poor compared with God that she was filled with humility. And so from this humble state she was lifted up to grace, and all manner of virtues and stands above all.[7] If commentary be needed it may be found in Julian's words: 'This above all causes the soul to seem small in its own sight: to see and love its maker. And this is what fills it with reverence and humility, and with generous love to our fellow-Christians.'[8]

*

Humility, as we have seen, is an elusive virtue, and if we try to capture it by direct assault we are liable to have the tables turned on us and to be left priding ourselves on the humility we suppose we have gained. It may be prudent to take the lowest seat at a feast, for it saves one from the embarrassment of being taken down a chair or two, but in so far as our motive is to advance in humility, in that degree will our design fail. Even so, we cannot do without the direct approach, and in the scriptural example I have chosen Jesus surely had more in mind than the exercise of worldly prudence. Indeed the Gospel writer indicates that this vivid little piece of teaching had direct application to humility: 'Everyone who exalts himself will be humbled; and whoever humbles himself will be exalted.' It is not in our power to do very much about our motives, but if we act in good faith in the best spirit that we can, God will accept and use our actions for the enrichment of both ourselves and others. Thus we should not belittle the importance of little sacrifices even if there is an element of self-consciousness in them. The imperfection of our state necessarily reveals itself in every action we undertake, in every word we utter, in every prayer we offer, in every step we walk, indeed in every breath we breathe. We are not to despise the little and homely remedies—it would in fact be a mark of pride to do so—such as restraining ourselves in conversation, curbing our natural curiosity, resisting the impulse to self-justification, doing little jobs cheerfully against our natural inclination, admitting our faults, being obedient (suspect though the word is today) to proper authority. The danger comes when we pursue the quest with such zeal that the self which needs to die is in a subtle and secret manner fed on what we are doing, and then under the guise of humility there may lurk an ugly pride. But that is to warn and not to ban. All such activities supply the opportunity for patience which may aptly be called the mother of humility, for it is indeed out of patience that humility is born.

All this, however, belongs to but the fringe of our subject and takes us only into the shallow waters. If the depths are to be plumbed it must be by the purging action of the Holy Spirit. Just as contemplative prayer has been divided into elements acquired and infused—a helpful division, though, as we shall see later, not entirely so—so we can usefully consider humility under these two heads. What has been said belongs to acquired humility; what we shall now consider belongs to that which is infused.

How is it that one may present the difference? It is the difference between owning oneself to be a wretch on the one hand, and on the other being patient and forbearing when that is how someone else sees one to be; or between making for oneself a rule of fasting as an ascetic discipline, and accepting patiently deprivation of food in, let us say, a refugee camp; or between denying oneself a television programme, and receiving patiently a caller just as one's favourite piece is under way. The list could be indefinitely extended, the distinction being that in the first case I initiate events and remain in

control, whereas in the second something is done to me outside my control, evoking from me one or another type of
response. Once we have shown ourselves ready to enter the
shallows, it will not be long before God summons us into
deeper waters. The progression which belongs to every committed Christian life is well illustrated in the words of Jesus
to Peter: 'When you were young you bound yourself and
walked wherever you wished; when you are old another shall
bind you and take you where you do not want to go.'[9]

Let us go more deeply into this cleansing action of the Holy
Spirit. A typical example will serve to illustrate our point. A
woman comes to see one—a committed Christian woman—
and she is troubled because when she moves into the silence
of prayer her imagination frequently becomes clouded with
thoughts of envy. What is she to do? One tells her that she
is to suffer patiently these thoughts to be there. One goes on
to explain that she is not to encourage them, not to search
them out and bring them to her mind. But equally import-
antly, once they have come she is not to attempt to drive
them away. She is to continue to wait silently upon God,
looking towards her centre, whether that is a word or sentence
held in the heart, or a visual aid such as an icon or a crucifix,
or some other point of focus. She will inevitably be aware of
her envious thoughts, but she is not to follow them nor vol-
untarily examine them, nor yet play tricks with herself, pre-
tending they are not there. This practice will be painful, but
she is to be content to suffer as she would be ready to suffer
a headache or some other physical pain. In acting in this
way, a gentle detachment from her envious thoughts will be
taking place, and it is likely that after a while they will leave
her. She is not happy (we shall suppose) about this advice at
first. Surely God cannot want this? Ought she not rather to
rise above these thoughts and drive them away? One replies
that it is probably because she has tried to push them away
in the past that they keep returning, probably with increased
force. It is painful for her to acknowledge her envious nature,
and as a result she is agitated and disturbed by it, but since
that is how it is, she must recognise it and accept it as
peacefully as she can, allowing her thoughts to be thus presented to the Holy Spirit for his healing work to be done, she

meanwhile suffering patiently each period of silence in which her condition recurs. Such an experience, patiently accepted and offered in union with Christ's passion, will inevitably work for the establishment within herself of a true and solid humility, and envy itself, being an offshoot of pride, will have no soil on which to feed.

It may be that our own affliction is not envy. Perhaps it is fear or anger or covetousness or aggression. But if we are on the same stage of the spiritual journey as the person of our example, the manner of dealing with it is the same. It may be of interest to note that Pusey writing to such a one troubled with sexual fantasies advises: 'Do not examine yourself about those thoughts whether you consented to them or not. Do not try not to have them. Be not impatient to get rid of them; only desire that you should love God more.' To suffer such thoughts patiently accepting yourself as you are, and looking in trustful surrender to God, is necessarily a humbling experience. For that very reason it is cleansing and healing. It was the teaching of the early fathers of the desert that we cannot fully acquire the virtue of purity until we have first acquired real humility of heart.

These words are spoken to those who are able to receive them. One may not so speak to every person. There are, as St Paul tells us, babes in Christ who are to be fed on milk, and those more mature who can take strong meat.[10] In psychological terms what has been written is for those in whom is formed, or is being formed; a stable ego centre. We shall speak more of this in a later chapter. In spiritual terms they are spoken to those who have been called to at least a moderately passive way of contemplative prayer; often it may be through the apprenticeship of the well-trodden discipline of discursive meditation. Once again we shall say more of that later on. Pusey's advice, for example, is no doubt excellent for the one to whom it was given. To another he might have advised that he should go and dig in the garden.

Spiritual direction, on the lines indicated, for what used to be called—one hears the phrase less often now—interior souls is deeply embedded in the Catholic tradition. Thus that great eighteenth-century French director Jean-Pierre de Caussade writes to a Sister of the Visitation:

16

To be in no way astonished at our wretchedness is a good foundation for humility based upon self-knowledge: while to feel that wretchedness keenly and constantly, and yet to be untroubled by it, is a very great grace from which springs distrust of self and true and perfect trust in God.[11]

Or moving on two centuries, and quoting from a passage bearing closely on the example we have taken, we find the much-sought-after Jesuit director Father Considine writing:

If (you) feel stirrings of jealousy . . . bear the jealous feelings quietly, and by degrees that will make you humble. If you pretend you have no such feelings you are rebelling against facts, and that is only a continuance of pride. You are on the high road to humility when you confess to yourself that you are horribly jealous and take it quietly. Be patient. You are so . . . don't get angry about it, accept it . . . You show you are very proud because you are in such a hurry to be humble.[12]

This then is what is meant by infused humility, the humility which is worked within as we are surrendered, passive, pliable in the hands of the Holy Spirit. Although the process has been described as experienced in the formal time of prayer, in reality no area of life is excluded. The Holy Spirit is thus acting to deepen and to heal as all life's frustrations, disappointments, sufferings, whether bodily or spiritual, are generously and lovingly offered. Often in suffering it is quite beyond our power to present the appearance of a heroic front either to others or to ourselves. This is the real humiliation of the situation. If only we could be like the resistance fighters under interrogation! Our cross may be to be little in the eyes of ourselves and those around us. God alone can know how it is with us. It is the pains which make our self-love suffer and the humiliations which crucify our pride which, at least in the middle areas of the spiritual life—not to be identified necessarily with the middle period of life—may provide the Holy Spirit with his best chance of doing his work in us. It is only self-will which can burn in hell, and once that is purged there is no fuel left to feed the fire. If this makes our faith look a matter of sorrow and gloom, it is probable that we have confused natural happiness with spiritual joy. It is not of course meant to exclude the many and probably more frequent glad and happy occasions of life which the Holy Spirit uses for the deepening of his own gifts within us. Perhaps indeed we would have more of them if we offered them as readily as our griefs. Our tendency is to hug them to ourselves instead of handing them over in a spirit of gratitude and praise.

*

Much of what has been written is not in the idiom of Julian. But it is all there in her own manner of presentation, and we have not moved away from the spirit of her thought. Thus she writes: 'He lays on each one he loves some particular thing, which while it carries no blame in his sight causes them to be blamed by the world, despised, scorned, mocked, and rejected.'[13] This, she goes on to explain, is that our pride may be overcome, and that united to Christ we may be made 'humble and mild, clean and holy'. In this our suffering 'our Lord rejoices with pity and compassion',[14] a line which must be linked with the following later in the chapter: 'For he wants us to know that it will all be turned to our honour and profit by the power of his Passion, and to know that we suffered in no way alone, but together with him, and to see in him our foundation.' Being united to Christ in his suffering is central to the whole work of redemption, and our chastisement itself 'becomes gentle and bearable when we are really content with him and with what he does . . .' 'What penance a man should impose upon himself was not revealed to me . . . but this was shown, with particular and loving emphasis, that we are to accept and endure humbly whatever penance God himself gives us with his blessed passion ever in mind.'[15] Julian adds that while we are to recognize and accept our chastening the remedy is 'that our Lord is with us, protecting and leading us into the fullness of joy'. And so we are taken to the climax of the chapter:

> Flee to our Lord and we shall be comforted. Touch him and we shall be made clean. Cling to him and we shall be safe and sound from every kind of danger. For our

courteous Lord wills that we should be as at home with him as heart may think or soul may desire.[16]

3

The Wrath is not in God

In the central chapters of her book Julian writes extensively on the subject of anger in God. 'I saw full surely that wherever our Lord appears, peace reigns, and anger has no place. For I saw no whit of anger in God in short or in long term.'[1] While Julian contents herself here with saying that she saw no anger in God, elsewhere she states firmly that there is no anger in God. 'God is that goodness which cannot be angry, for God is nothing but goodness.'[2] Julian wrestles with this question here and in the following chapters. She does not eliminate the idea of wrath altogether but teaches that it is on man's side and not on God's, and she describes it as 'a perversity and an opposition to peace and love'.[3] This, in turn, she describes as 'a lack of power or a lack of wisdom or a lack of goodness, and this lack is not in God, but it is on our side. For we through sin and wretchedness have in us a wrath and a constant opposition to peace and love.' It is, if we may use a simple analogy, as though a number of children drink from a common supply of milk. Whereas most are nourished, several become ill. The milk—as is God's love—is the same for all, but there is that within these few children which for them turns it into something like poison. St Catherine of Sienna tells how at the last judgement all will look upon the face of Christ. The saved will behold it with joy, the lost with terror. But, she adds, it is the same face they all look upon.

St Paul is making the same point in the first epistle to the Corinthians when he writes that those who eat the body and blood of Christ unworthily do so to their own judgement.[4] It is one gift for all but it may be that our perversity will turn it into condemnation.

Our lives will be enriched according to the measure to which we are able to understand and penetrate with heart as well as mind Julian's 'shewing' at this point. It may be that nothing that Julian writes should engage our attention more than this teaching, which is central to her book. An earlier chapter gives us the key which interprets her thought: 'Peace and love are always alive in us, but we are not always alive to peace and love.'[5] At every stage the hindrance is to be found in ourselves and not in God. If when I have fallen, I know that there is nothing within God which has to change, but only within me, then I may at once receive in faith the forgiveness which in God's eyes is already mine. If, in a family situation, a child has done some wrong and turns to his father for forgiveness, there can only be frustration and grief if he sees his father's face turned in anger against him. Our point is that we never have to feel that way with God. 'It is his will and counsel that we should stay with him, and hold ourselves closely to him for ever . . . for whether we are clean or foul it is all one to his love.'[6] God's face of compassionate love is always turned towards us, and if what we see in God is wrath, that is because of a corruption within ourselves which we have projected on to God, for our tendency is always to make God in our own image. But that is not where wrath belongs: it is our projection only. The sun *is* shining. I can perhaps neither see it nor feel its warmth, the reason being (if we may continue this rather crude illustration) that after passing through the wind and the storm, I have my umbrella still above my head. The fault is in me. I know myself to be a fool, but the remedy is close at hand.

Before we pass on it will be interesting to note that Martin Luther illustrates Julian's point in speaking of his relationship with his confessor. 'Sometimes', he writes, 'my confessor said to me when I repeatedly discussed silly sins with him, "You are a fool. God is not incensed against you, but you are incensed against God. God is not angry with you, but you are angry with God." ' And Luther comments: 'This was magnificently said.'[7]

*

Julian states emphatically that there is no wrath in God, and it may be instructive to ask the nature of the wrath she is concerned to deny. In chapter 46 Julian writes:

> And yet in all this time, from the beginning to the end, I had two kinds of contemplation. The one was endless continuing love, with certainty of protection and blessed salvation, for all the revelation was about this. The other was the common teaching of Holy Church, in which before I had been instructed and grounded, and had by my will practised and understood.[8]

With the above passage quoted apart from its context, it might be thought to have bearing on contemplative prayer. Julian is not, however, using 'contemplation' in that sense. Her mind at this stage is sharply and painfully occupied with the concepts of wrath and mercy, and she is saying that she is conscious of two levels of awareness. The first springs from her 'shewings'; and this level is typified by 'endless continuing love' and is an area where wrath in God has no place at all. The second level reaches her through the teaching of the Church, and here she finds the emphasis to be on judgement and wrath to come. God (and Jesus too) had come to be regarded as a harsh judge who would at the last exercise vengeance and retribution on those who had failed to meet his stern demands. That is not, of course, the only side. The Church, as always, mediated forgiveness to those who repented of their sins, but even here joy and assurance were undermined by the offer being presented conditionally upon the performance of good works of penance by which God's anger might be appeased or his favour won. There is no peace to be found down that road, as St Paul so clearly saw: 'For by grace are you saved through faith: and that not of yourselves: it is the gift of God: not of works lest any man should boast.'[9]

Into this climate of theological cheerlessness and doom Julian's message burst like a joyous song. If the image of God were seriously distorted her 'even-Christians' could not but be the victims of hopelessness and despair. But everything that she 'saw' witnessed to a God far removed from the popular conception around her. His graciousness, she pleaded, could be counted upon on all the occasions of life, and not least in our 'failing' and 'falling' and 'dying', for here too 'the sweet eye of pity is never turned away from us, and the operation of mercy does not cease'.[10] In all such times, she would have her 'even-Christians' know, God looks upon us 'with pity and not with blame'.[11] Moreover we are not to be surprised, nor depressed, nor discouraged by occasions of falling, for what at least is certain is that we can never fall outside God's love. Our falling, Julian might well have said, is not so much a falling into sin as a falling into the arms of God's mercy.

> Though we sin continually he loves us endlessly, and so gently does he shew us our sin that we repent of it quietly, turning our mind to the contemplation of his mercy, clinging to his love and goodness, knowing that he is our cure, understanding that we do nothing but sin . . . (For) if there be anywhere on earth a lover of God who is always kept safe from falling, I know nothing of it—for it was not shown me. But this was shown: that in falling and rising again we are always held close in one love.[12]

And so it is (she has written earlier) that 'mercy works protecting, enduring, vivifying and healing, and it is all of the tenderness of love; and grace works with mercy . . . (transforming) our dreadful failing into plentiful and endless solace . . . our shameful falling into high and honourable rising . . . our sorrowful dying into holy, blessed life.'[13] Yet the conflict raged on, on the one hand the teaching of the 'shewings', on the other that of 'Holy Church' in which Julian's faith was grounded. She could not rest 'because of great fear and perplexity'.[14] To her 'astonishment' her visions had shown that God attached 'no more blame to us than if we were as pure and holy as the angels are in heaven'. Yet the Church taught, and her own feelings had at this stage confirmed, that God's 'blame' had rested on her and all men 'from the first man until the time that we come up into heaven'. It was for Julian an agony parallel to that of St Paul, and echoing the words of the apostle—'O wretched man that I am, who shall deliver me . . .'[15]—she cries within herself, with all her 'might' beseeching God's help, 'Ah Lord Jesus, King of bliss, how shall

I be comforted, who will tell me and teach me what I need to know, if I cannot at this time see it in you?' There followed the revelation of the lord and the servant. Julian must be allowed to introduce it in the beauty of her own words:

I saw two persons in bodily form: a lord and a servant . . . The lord is seated in solemn state, at rest and in peace. The servant is standing by his lord respectfully, ready to do his master's will. With love, gracious and tender, the lord looks upon his servant, and sends him on an errand to a certain place. Not only does the servant go, but he darts off at once, running at great speed, for love's sake, to do his master's bidding. Almost at once he falls into a ditch and hurts himself badly. He moans and groans, cries out and struggles, but he cannot get up or help himself in any way. Yet, as I saw it, his greatest trial was that there was no comfort at hand; for he was unable so much as to turn his face to look upon his loving lord, in whom is full comfort; and this, although he was very close to him. Instead, behaving weakly and foolishly for the time being, he thought only of his grief and distress. . . .

I marvelled how this servant could meekly suffer such distress, and I looked carefully to see if I could discover any fault in him, or if his master should assign any blame. But I saw none: for the only cause of his fall was his good-will and his eagerness. He was now in spirit just as willing and good as when he had stood before his lord ready to do his will.[16]

It is a homely picture of ourselves. Eager to do God's work, and perhaps moving too hastily, we have stumbled badly and come to grief. To crown our sufferings we seem for a while to be separated from God, and his face to be hidden from us. Yet that is to see things only from our side, and, leaving out the mercy and compassion of God, it is hardly surprising if we fall into despondency and despair. So it is that Julian paints the other side of the picture, the part of the canvas we are to see in faith, however much mood and emotion may be acting against us. Looking now to the master she tells us that not only does he assign no blame, but that he looks on his fallen servant 'very lovingly and gently, with great compassion and pity'. But there is more, and here is a lovely Julian touch. The master was planning for the future, delighting in the reward he had in mind for this loyal and devoted man. He was saying to himself, and Julian's own words will say it best:

> See my beloved servant here, what hurt and distress he has endured in service for love of me—and of his good-will. Is it not fitting that I should reward him for his fright and fear, his pain and his wounds, and all his grief? And not only this. Should I not award him a gift which would serve him better, and be more excellent than his own health would have been? Surely it would be ungracious not to do this.

It is a picture which proclaims the overwhelming generosity of God. I recall reading many years ago—I cannot now trace where—a sermon on the parable of the prodigal son, showing how at every point God's love exceeds our expectations. The dispirited boy made his way home hoping his father would receive him; instead he was met and welcomed and embraced. He hoped for clothing to replace his tattered rags; he finds the best robe brought out and put upon him. Longing for a meal to satisfy his hunger, he hears a feast proclaimed in his honour. Content to be allowed to work as a servant, he finds that his sonship has never lapsed. It is strangely true that while we can understand and accept such magnanimity at a human level it is often more difficult—perhaps due to our early conditioning—to accept it in God. But 'God is a good man',[17] and the charity to which we can but dimly reach is rooted in his very being.

Here then is a comfortable doctrine, comfortable in the old meaning of the word, not snug and cosy but full of encouragement, consolation and strength. Julian's emphasis and presentation make real and vivid an important truth. Her insistence that God's love rests upon us, and goes on resting upon us in spite of anything we in our blindness or perversity or ignorance may do, is a much needed message for our growth in Christ. Though we are faithless God's compassionate love remains. Our falling does not hinder him from loving us. Julian insists on the importance of our understanding this.

*

Closely linked with our thinking in this chapter is Julian's observation that we must learn to forgive ourselves. This is an insight we are likely to be more aware of today than was general in earlier generations, for psychologists make the point that no one can truly love another (or love God) so long as he hates himself. Aelred of Rievaulx has a trinity of loves, saying that every time we love God more, it follows, and it must follow, that we love our neighbour more, and (in the deepest sense) ourselves more. So too the true love of our neighbour automatically means increased love of God and self. And the love of self in the fullest long-term sense must be for the increase of the love of God and our neighbour. Jesus tells us that we have to learn to love our neighbour as ourselves, which means, among other things, that we have to learn to accept ourselves with the same generosity with which we would accept another, blemishes, quirks, weaknesses and all. Julian sees this clearly: If God forgives us, who are we to withhold forgiveness from ourselves? 'As by his courtesy God forgives our sins when we repent, even so he wills that we should forgive our sin, and so give up our senseless worrying and faithless fear';[18] and again, 'nor does he will that we should busy ourselves too much with self-accusation; nor is it his will that we should despise ourselves. But he wills that we should quickly turn to him.'[19] Yet again, 'He says, "do not blame yourself too much, thinking that your trouble and distress is all your fault. For it is not my will that you should be unduly sad and despondent." '[20] Our despondency is a favourite aim of the enemy who 'tries to depress us by false fears which he proposes. His intention is to make us so weary and dejected that we let the blessed sight of our everlasting friend slip from our minds.'

The acceptance of ourselves and one another as we are is an important truth, but it may need qualification if it is not to be misunderstood. It is commonly said that God loves us as we are, and that that is how we should love our neighbour and ourselves. There is truth in this but it is not the whole truth; for we are living persons and destined to grow in ever fuller measure into the stature of Christ. A man may not love a living thing in the same way that he loves an inanimate object. I love a favourite picture as it is, and shall dust it tomorrow that it may remain as it is today. I have too a favourite plant and I love that too for what it is (at this particular instant), but I shall water it that it may become what now it is not. God's love for us is clearly analogous to a man's love for his plant, and a right love for ourselves follows the same pattern. In accepting ourselves as we are, we acknowledge that this is how God would at this instant have us to be, but we do not forget the continuing watering of his grace which is destined to carry us not simply to where we are not, but beyond any horizons we can now imagine.

The ground of our salvation is in God, and perhaps no writer presents this concept more compellingly than does Julian in her *Revelations*. Especially is this true when she comes to write of the motherhood of God. In chapter 59 she writes that 'as truly as God is our father, so just as truly is he our mother',[21] and in the following chapter she speaks of 'our true mother Jesus, who is all love, and bears us into joy and endless living'.[22] As a mother feeds her child with her milk so 'our beloved mother Jesus feeds us with himself' and 'in tender courtesy he gives us the Blessed Sacrament, the treasured food of life'. As for ourselves, we are like small children watched over and learning to walk. 'We need to fall and we need to see that we have done so. For if we never fell we should not know how weak and pitiable we are in ourselves. Nor should we fully know the wonderful love of our maker.'[23] Yet when we fall we are to know that 'he holds us lovingly and graciously and swiftly raises us.'[24] Jesus is likened to 'a kind nurse who has no other care but the welfare of her child'. And Julian adds that 'it is his responsibility to save us, it is his glory to do so, and it is his will that we should know it'. Thus the initiative is always with God, whose patience and inexhaustible love are active towards us at all times.

4

Falling We Stand

'In God's sight we do not fall, in our sight we do not stand.
As I see it both of these are true. But the deeper insight
belongs to God.'[1] Julian is writing, as always, for her 'even-
Christians', for 'those-who-shall-be-saved', and we do well to
consider her deeply at this point. Taken together with the
teaching of the last chapter, we have here an insight which
may encourage us on every stage of our journey. We shall
need this and the next chapter to draw out its meaning, and
its application to the spiritual life.

I think that what Julian is saying may be interpreted
broadly along two distinct lines. These we may take in turn.
For the first, or as an example of the first, let me recount an
experience from my own life. It happened during a retreat I
was conducting at a convent. I had been through a day of
considerable mental and spiritual conflict, and I knew that
the evening address would not be easy. I was, however, little
prepared for what actually happened. After speaking to the
Sisters for five or ten minutes I broke down and wept as I sat
there in the conductor's chair. Had they been tears of compassion or joy or penitence, it would perhaps have been quite
easy—I believe the Curé d'Ars experienced such in many
sermons. It was certainly none of these but something much
less respectable: exhaustion, or depression, or self-pity perhaps. I do not know. The nuns, as you may expect, were
sensible enough just to sit there quietly and wait, and perhaps
pray, and after a minute or two, knowing it was impossible
to continue the address, I read two letters from de Caussade's
Self Abandonment to the Divine Providence which was at my side.
People who know me well can witness to my proud nature,
and if further evidence were needed it was supplied by the

smarting humiliation I felt that night. I had not come across Julian at that time, but now that I know her writings I find her words appropriate to just such an incident: 'In your eyes you do not stand, in God's eyes you do not fall. I see both to be true but God's insight is the deeper.' For this happening, which seemed to me to have about it all the marks of a miserable failure, was, I believe, a breakthrough. Looking back I can see that a little bit of the hard shell of pride was pierced that night, and that the experience was in fact to be seen in God's providence as being for my growth and not my undoing. And God, who never does things by halves, seemed to make it right for the Sisters too, for one of them said later— her eagerness to console perhaps outrunning her sensitivity— that the letters which I read were the best part of the retreat. After that there wasn't too much of me left.

That little incident stands for what may so often happen to us. We have our ideals, our standards, an image of ourselves, perhaps, to which we want to conform, even more an image of how we appear to others, which it would be very painful to have destroyed. And in all this we know there is a good deal of pride and complacency and self-will. Then something happens—an outburst of temper or impatience or bitterness it may be—and this image is destroyed, and it seems to us that we have fallen badly. At such times it may be well to recall Julian's words: 'In your eyes you do not stand, in God's eyes you do not fall. I see both to be true but God's insight is the deeper one.' For what in fact has happened? Almost certainly our 'goodness' or 'good works' have proceeded too much from some outward standard we have set for ourselves, and too little from the love which springs from being united to God in faith and hope. Our good works have borne as little resemblance to the fruit of the Spirit as the plastic apples and grapes you sometimes see bear to the real thing, though there is an outward and superficial likeness which may for the time deceive. And if our 'fall' serves to undermine our false self-confidence, if it breaks up the hard ground of self-satisfaction and leads us once more as little children to throw all our confidence on God, to abandon ourselves anew into his arms, then, although it may seem like a fall to us, to God it is perhaps the breakthrough into reality he has been waiting for.

There is a story of a father whose small daughter had been very ill in hospital. At one time it is thought that she will not recover, but then the news is better, and on the way to visit her he buys a splendid chocolate cake hoping she may soon be well enough to enjoy it. On reaching the hospital he goes first to the chapel, where he kneels in silent thanksgiving before the crucifix. When, however, he arrives at the hospital ward, a nurse meets him to say his child has had a relapse and died. He makes his way back to the chapel and, standing before the crucifix, he flings the cake bitterly at the figure on the cross. Of course it is an outrageous thing to do, yet may we not say that he who bore the nails found it not all that difficult to absorb a chocolate cake? But what a humiliation, what a lot of explaining and apologies the next day! And yet it could be that in that little chapel, there was poured out the poison and the resentment harboured secretly for many years, and that God, who knows us so much better than we know ourselves, welcomed the outburst as breaking up hard and fallow ground, making it possible for the waters of healing to flow.[2]

I suppose that most convents have suffered at one time or another from having among them the perfect novice. You know the sort of person I mean. Everything is done just right. She is punctual and tidy and faithful in her duties. Her obedience cannot be faulted. In but a few days she has mastered the intricacies of the office book. She never forgets to light the altar candles, nor to put out the convent cat at night. Then it happens! The strain of it all catches up on her, and like a poor, frightened, exhausted child she breaks down in front of the community. Or it may be that she creates some fearful scene in public which is deeply revealing and humiliating to her. And Mother Superior, however she may appear outwardly, in an interior manner of speaking throws up her arms and cries 'Hurrah', and reflects that Novice Amanda may make it after all. I think that that is the sort of thing we may take out of Julian's saying, God throwing up his arms and crying 'Hurrah' just when we think we have made the most frightful mess of everything. She says, indeed, something very much like it in chapter 28, though she reminds us that God's rejoicing is tempered with compassion.

*

Julian's words may also be applied in a quite different way. We may take them as having application in the conflict every Christian passes through in putting on his liberty in Christ. We all long to be free, but often we are chained to ways of doing things, and looking at things, and understanding things, which may have served us well enough in the past, but now instead of promoting our growth to completeness in Christ it may well be that they impede it. This was the journey which St Paul had to make, and with what courage and imaginative vision he made it, the journey from Pharisaism of the most strict and rigid kind, hedged in by rules and rituals which covered the minutest details of everyday life, to the freedom he describes as the heritage of the children of God. Our legalisms today are not, at least for the most part, those known to Saul of Tarsus, but we probably find it as difficult to break through the things which bind us as did any Jew brought up under the ancient law. And if when the call comes we do not respond because it is painful or fearful, then our lives individually and corporately become stunted, impeding our growth into the fullness of Christ. An example from the New Testament may first be taken to illustrate our meaning.

Many an early Christian from a strictly Jewish background must have been plagued with feelings of guilt in the early stages of eating with the Gentiles—polluted food as he had been brought up to believe. Imagine such a one faced with the prospect of eating for the first time at a Gentile meal. On the one hand he knew it was no sin, that is to say he knew it with his head, for had not Jesus pronounced all meats clean? Yet everything within him produced by years of training, upbringing and teaching rebelled at what he was about to do. We may trace it in Peter, and no one had more opportunity of knowing the mind of his master than he. He must have already made some progress when the dream came for he was staying with Simon, a tanner, who in Jewish eyes was following an unclean trade and hence had to be housed outside the main part of the city. Peter, who had broken through sufficiently to lodge with this fellow-Christian, falls asleep one hot day on the roof of Simon's sea-side house. The smell of cooking has probably reached him from below, and perhaps his last sight was of the ships in billowing sail across the water. And so it is that as he sleeps a sheet full of all kinds of meats descends, and a voice says to him, 'Rise, Peter; kill, and eat.' Usually we can be more free in dreams than in waking life, but with Peter the repression has gone deep, and everything within him rises to protest: 'Not so, Lord; for I have never eaten anything that is common or unclean.' It was not until the vision was repeated for the third time that the message won through: 'What God has cleansed, you must not call common.' And so he is made free, or for the time being at least (for, as we know, his doubts returned),[3] and he is able to go to the house of Cornelius and with a directness of speech which may sound somewhat harsh to us today, tell him that God had taught him that he must regard no man as common or unclean. Hence freedom was won, and the Church was launched on a course enabling it to embrace all men everywhere, instead of remaining a sect within Judaism which might have died within a hundred years.[4]

Our own movements into freedom are less momentous for history, but it is likely that they are as real and difficult for ourselves. It is important that we should understand what we are doing. A story relates how Jesus came across a man gathering sticks on the Sabbath. This was a serious infringement of the law and the penalty was severe. Jesus told him that if he knew what he was doing he was blessed, but that if he did not know he was cursed. If this man was breaking the rules with a bad conscience, that could be no blessing to him. But if he had come to see that God was not the taskmaster he had been brought up to believe, but a loving father who had made the Sabbath for man, then the work he was doing revealed a breakthrough from law to grace, and took him on a blessed journey. We are not to act against our consciences but we often have to make the discovery that what we have taken to be our conscience is not in fact the voice of God speaking within us, but some other voice; the voice, perhaps, of our early conditioning, or of some authority figure in the past; or of social convention, or of pride; or, not least, the voice of our super-ego—harsh, bullying and exacting it may well be. Where among these conflicting claimants does the voice of God lie?

If we return to the case of Peter, then so long as he was a Jew there was no conflict in his mind about foods. The rules were laid down, and he had only to observe them. This is a safe and comfortable situation, but it constitutes a bondage and so a threat to growth. The liberty in Christ lay ahead, and to enter that liberty is to find peace, a deeper and more solid peace than before. But what of the transition period? This is the time which is marked by pain and conflict, anxiety, doubt and fear. It then needs courage to go forward. These are the times when in our sight we may not stand, yet in God's sight we do not fall. We may pass through them assured in the mind that we are right, yet at another level guilt feelings arise, and although we may know them to be morbid that does not lessen their pain.

To one who has not known the type of experience through which the early Christians had to pass as they put on their liberty in Christ, transcending the regulations of Judaism— to such a one it may be impossible to understand the pain and conflict involved. Yet every committed Christian must, I fancy, pass through a similar experience in finding liberty from the disabling restrictions which his background and upbringing, and not infrequently the Church herself, have placed upon him.

I may illustrate by an example, and from there we may extend our thinking. Women of the generation immediately preceding the Second World War, and yet more of generations before that, found it very difficult, or even impossible, to enter a church building if not wearing a hat. Yet, no matter what the tradition of the centuries had been, they would almost certainly have been aware that God could not possibly be so small as to give or withhold his blessing according to the presence or absence of hat or veil. Even so, it would be true to say for most church women that if, believing as they did, they had forced themselves to go through the motions and to spend a while in church with the head uncovered, guilt feelings would arise, and the ensuing conflict would effectively scatter any peace of mind they had hoped to find. If we men find that strange, we have only to reverse the procedure, and see ourselves before the altar with hat on head, not out of bravado, but for the very good reason of keeping our heads warm in our cold churches. Of course God could not be so petty, and yet. . .? But to return, we may say women were right to go forward and, morbid guilt feelings subsiding after a while, a new area of freedom was won. The point we have to note, and it will recur frequently as our thought develops, is that there would at first have been an appearance of evil in what it was proposed to do. Probably for most the evil would have presented itself as an act of irreverence to God, though some more instructed ones might have seen it as disobedience to scriptural teaching arrived at by the somewhat tortuous arguments of St Paul.[5] Whichever way it was, the guilt feelings would be there and that is all that is relevant to our immediate purpose. Yet how such women stood in their own eyes was not a correct assessment. In God's eyes, we shall confidently affirm, they did not fall.

An example of greater moment, and one which affects us all, may be found in considering the manner in which we express our allegiance to truth. That we should always speak the truth, and that it is wrong to tell a lie, has probably been a part of our Christian training from earliest years. Perhaps no part of a child's upbringing is of greater importance than this precept, but it needs to be taught with sympathetic understanding, and if the direction is interpreted too rigidly it may make for serious problems later on. For the fact is that our relationship to truth is expressed better in the words of Jesus, 'I have come to bear witness to the truth',[6] than in the speaking of the truth as we commonly understand those words. Happily the two normally coincide, but when they are in conflict it is how we may best bear witness to the truth which we must try to decide. Thus if a father 'tells a lie' to conceal his child's whereabouts from a man brandishing a knife, it would not be correct to say that truth for the moment had been set aside, but rather that truth had been vindicated because the deeper truth in this situation is that life is sacred and is not to be placed at the disposal of evil men. The example is extreme but the principle it illustrates belongs to many life situations. Bonhoeffer argues in his *Ethics* that if a boy, who is asked by his teacher in front of the class if his father comes home drunk at night, replies 'untruthfully' that he does not, then truth has been vindicated because the boy has witnessed to the deeper truth, that a teacher has no right to ask such questions before the class.[7] It may often happen with good people that they are troubled by a lie, when in fact they have borne faithful witness to the deeper rather than the superficial truth of a situation.[8] Yet this lie is on their conscience—'in their eyes they do not stand'—and the need is for them to break through the legalistic conception of 'telling the truth' into the freedom of bearing witness to the truth which lies beyond.

It is obvious that what has been said could be applied to a great variety of situations involving people in all walks of life. Doctors and nurses have to come to terms with our question in a great variety of ways, involving often an agony of decision. The deeper truth is not always the literal one, and to bear witness to it is demanding. A myth may be a powerful instrument of the truth, and parents and teachers often bear witness to that in the teaching of children. Let it not be said that we are at any point arguing that the end justifies the means, but rather that we are trying to see how truth may best be witnessed to in different situations. Our problem is that we insist on fastening legalistic conceptions on to God, thereby curtailing the liberty in which Christ would have us move. Thus indeed it happens in a variety of situations that in our sight we do not stand, though we may believe that a deeper insight which belongs to God is awaiting us.

We could take many examples, some of a bygone generation and others with us today, where legalistic conceptions fastened on to God by teaching or tradition may curtail our freedom in Christ. We certainly could neither love nor respect a man or woman who imposed upon us the restrictions sometimes attributed to God. Matters which used to exercise us in the Church fifty years ago are happily seldom live issues today. But many vexed questions remain, as most of us are probably painfully aware. Our need is to remember that whenever we raise a practice or precept—invaluable as it may be for the time being as a devotional or practical aid—to the level of a principle seen mistakenly as grounded in the very being of God, we become idolaters within the strict meaning of the word.[9] Even so it must be that in some measure we are all idolaters, for who can search out the mind of God? Yet search we must, and if our searching means the undermining of our earlier ways of acting and thinking, then we must go forward with such courage as is given us. And as we painfully and gropingly make our way, sometimes along paths which our training and background, and it may be the traditions of the Church, have led us to believe we may not tread, it may often seem to us that we do not stand, whereas to God may belong the deeper insight that we do not fall. Clearly Julian's saying can be manipulated to selfish ends; but for those who have discovered her that is not likely to be so. Our need rather is to explore with hope and courage the lights God has brought to our generation, and to take her words as giving boldness to go forward where we might otherwise have held back.

Two Hindrances to Freedom

In the last chapter we took Julian's words: 'In God's sight we do not fall, in our sight we do not stand. As I see it both of these are true, but the deeper insight belongs to God.' Julian has somewhat similar words earlier in her book: 'For God looks at things in one way, and man looks at them in another. It is natural for man humbly to accuse himself, and it is natural for the proper goodness of God graciously to excuse man.'[1] We were considering our passage in the context of our growth to freedom in Christ, and we may now ask what it is which holds us back, thereby stunting our growth and preventing us from becoming our true selves as we exist and have existed from eternity in the mind of God.

Let us explore two things which may stand in our way. The first is the tendency we may have to identify ourselves with our persona. The persona, which is a term used widely by Jung, is in reality the actor's mask, and as Jung says it is necessary for every man and woman to have a persona. Possibly we can grasp this point best if we see the persona as being literally something to do with the stage. Every actor has his rôle, and for the period of the play he is identified with it—the hero, the villain, the comedian, or whatever it may be. This is right, and a man or woman would be a bad actor if it were otherwise. The trouble comes when a person comes to identify himself with his rôle. This identification may be more or less conscious, and the more conscious it is the less is the harm done. Indeed, fully conscious identification is harmless, as it may be for the actor on the stage. It is as this identification becomes unconsciously assumed that the trouble sets in. We may illustrate this by taking as an example the case of a circus clown. Here then he is, plain John Smith, and for a period each afternoon and evening he is Bimbo the clown acting his clever and funny part to one enthralled audience after another. So far all is well. But it could well be that after some years of this regular routine John Smith disappears and Bimbo the clown takes over. John Smith goes to a party, and it is second nature to him to clown his way through—indeed it has come to be expected of him. This is where the danger lies; the man is on his way to becoming his persona. But let it be said again that the danger is lessened in so far as John Smith remains conscious that he is putting on an act, that he is not really the funny man he is impersonating.

We all have a persona and we all need to have a persona. The doctor, for example, is a doctor-figure, in his white coat and with the paraphernalia of the surgery around him, and we call him Dr Robinson and give him the trust and honour due to his position, and probably we have much more confidence in him as a doctor than does his wife who knows him as a husband, or his children who know him as a father. The nurse has her persona, or the headmaster, or the sergeant-major, or the Queen—whoever it may be. And this is right. But once any of them moves towards unconsciously identifying himself with his persona, once the sergeant-major slips into becoming within the family the authoritarian figure he quite rightly becomes on the parade-ground, then there is trouble. The personality will tend to remain static within the self-chosen rôle, or to develop along the lines the rôle requires of it.

Fortunately the sergeant-major is helped by the fact that when he comes off parade, or at least off duty, he will remove his uniform and change into mufti. Thus he does not have to carry around with him all day the external badge of his office. The same is true of the policeman, or the hospital nurse, or the ticket inspector, or many other authority-figures. The priest is, or rather was, less fortunate; for until recent years he was expected at all times to wear clothing which identified him with his calling. In the case of the monk or nun tradition—at least in the Anglican orders—is dying more slowly. The habitual wearing of the priestly or religious uniform is not necessarily crippling or damaging—and there are many compensating advantages—but the danger of unconscious identification with the persona remains. James Smith is liable to disappear, and to become Father Smith unknowingly identifying himself with his image of the priestly rôle, or with the considerably distorted image society places upon it. Mary Jane as God wanted her to be can become lost in the ample folds of Sister Annabella's habit. The image of what the calling requires can so dominate the outlook as to present a threat to growth to freedom in Christ; and where that is inhibited personality remains static. The full working through of this process will do great harm. It is partly with this possibility in view that some communities like their members to have periods, such as holidays, when the uniform is discarded. For this period they may go into a shop or restaurant or theatre or railway train and be simply themselves with no superimposed rôle to carry around with them. Admittedly there is loss as well as gain; and from the practical and economic point of view it may be demanding. Its value is best assessed by clergy and religious who have known both ways.

*

A second factor which may well inhibit growth is what psychologists call an over-rigid ego-structure. This is a failing which is liable to belong not to this or that occupation but, so far as it is lawful to generalize, to people of an older generation whatever their profession may be. Probably we are to find its origins in the way many of us have been brought up. Often this has been within rigid structures, and a good deal of ourselves may have been repressed lest we break the code of conduct accepted by those around us, or too easily cross the boundaries of convention. Archbishop Coggan once said to Synod, 'Thank God for tradition; it gives you guidelines.' But he was quick to add, 'Beware of tradition, it can throttle you.' We do not question the value of tradition, but we have to acknowledge that freedom and spontaneity may be casualties on the way. But whereas the older ones among us may have been hedged in by many rules when we were young, a younger generation brought up in a much freer atmosphere—it may sometimes be too free—has sometimes lost its bearings and become confused, anchorless and unstuck. If the problem of an older generation has been that of an over-rigidified ego, that of the younger has sometimes been the failure to form a stable and developed ego, and in such cases conscious life is likely to be swamped and overwhelmed by forces which cannot be controlled. The ill-developed ego may be likened to the desert sands, shapeless and ill-defined, taking one form after another according to the wind which blows. A weak and immature ego places a man at the mercy of his instinct and emotions; he cannot preserve his integrity against the pressure of fashion and popular opinion and becomes the ready victim of life-styles which offer quick returns, but no lasting remedies. Yet no less disastrous is the over-rigid ego, the uninviting, hard and rocky surface, secure and well-defined, incapable of modifying its outlines in a changing and developing world.

Between these two states, the over-rigid and the ill-developed ego, lies the properly developed ego—the firm yet workable soil, if we return to our illustration—to be roughly equated with stability and strength of character, taking the ego to be that which rules the conscious mind. Jung stresses the necessity of establishing a stable and well-developed ego if the unconscious elements in our nature are to be properly handled. Thus during youth ego development should be stressed, or the attempt to integrate unconscious elements into the conscious life may lead simply to the swamping of the conscious self, leaving it at the mercy of the emerging forces. In an older generation this development was stressed—over-stressed it may often have been. In his contribution to *The Great Christian Centuries to Come*[2] Martin Thornton uses the following sets of seven words to illustrate the difference in background of Christians of an older and younger generation: Morality, duty, discipline, method, application, self-control, 'seriousness'. Love, spontaneity, abandonment, freedom, experiment, self-expression, gaiety. It will be seen that these fourteen words will pair with one another, morality with love, duty with spontaneity and so on. If we have been brought up exclusively on the first seven words the danger is that we shall freeze. And if we have been brought up exclusively on the last seven the danger is that we shall drown. We need always to be moving into a balance suited to our stage in life.

But it is the over-rigid ego we are now trying to identify. The Jungian analyst and writer Karlfried Von-Durkheim gives four marks of the over-rigid ego.[3] We may set them out as follows:

(1) A *stubborn* clinging to the established order.
(2) An acute suffering in many things which involve change.
(3) A need to defend oneself if threatened by change by entrenching oneself more obstinately in the system one has been accustomed to.
(4) An itch for perfection.

While we may have anticipated the first three of the marks given, the fourth may at first sight seem surprising, for it has about it the appearance of what is good and noble. Deeper reflection will, however, reveal that perfectionism may be in conflict with that complete surrender of oneself which is content to see the work of sanctification done in God's time and in God's way. The fact is that perfectionism is commendable when understood adverbially, dangerous when seen adjectivally. Interpreting that riddle, we might say that Jesus the carpenter never made perfect tables (perfect being an adjective), but that he always made tables perfectly. He may not have made perfect tables because the wood was inadequate, or the tools imperfectly suited, or the time insufficient, and so on. But he made tables perfectly in that the complete offering of his skills marked everything that he did. So our perfection is to be found in the fullness of the offering rather than in whether the flowers we plant grow, or the bread turns out well, or the singing is in tune, though naturally we do our best within the limits open to us. The same is true in relation to conduct. It is not a matter of being able to reach some objective standard of excellence, but rather of the desire to be open fully to the inflow of the Holy Spirit as God enables us.

The breaking up of the over-rigid ego is never without suffering. We shall experience this each time we break through a tenaciously held opinion, firmly adhered to, it may be, for many years, and so move into an area of greater freedom. As we reach the critical point it will generally seem to us that the thing we now propose to do, or the way of thinking we are coming to adopt, will have about it the nature of evil. Peter's vigorous and impassioned protest, 'Not so, Lord, for I have never eaten anything which is common or unclean', is likely to be ours, rephrased to suit the particular situation which confronts us. Thus the ardent teetotaller, having moved to a more liberal position, is not likely to be spared the feelings of guilt as he prepares to take his first drink.[4] Or take the case of the Sabbatarian who, after a childhood and youth of conditioning, contemplates his first game of cricket on a Sunday. No wonder if he so shakes at the wicket as to succumb to the first ball. I recall one such who was only able to join in a game of Scrabble on Sundays by insisting that only words in the Bible might be chosen. Or consider the fundamentalist who has for many years insisted on the literal inerrancy of the Christian or other Scriptures. As he breaks through to a deeper and more spiritual approach will it not seem that God's displeasure is upon him? Or finally reflect on the desperate dilemma of the Jehovah's Witness parents as they learn that only a blood transfusion will save their 'dying' child. Giving their consent after an agonizing period of prayer and indecision, and finding the whole weight of their worshipping community against them, it may well seem that the heavens will open and swallow them up. Yet what have these people done but laid hold on the freedom in which Christ would set them free?

We may extend our examples to many questions which exercise Christian minds in the Church today. We have the issues of divorce and remarriage in church, of women priests and deacons, of the celibacy of the priesthood, of the validity of one another's orders, to mention only ecclesiastical matters, and of them but a few. To these may be added a host of questions within the field of personal, social and medical ethics. Our purpose now is not to attempt to assess the merit of one position over another, but simply to make the point that whenever we have stubbornly clung to one side of a question, and then in the face of further light have loosened our hold to move into a fuller freedom in Christ, the thing we contemplate will at first be likely to have about it the appearance of evil.[5]

If we look back to Durkheim's guide-lines, we shall see that the second mark of the over-rigid ego is the acute suffering to be expected in the presence of change. We have already noted and discussed one reason why this will be so. A further suffering will, however, arise from the threatened destruction of our self-image, and yet more in the overthrow of the image which others have formed of us. This is a severe blow to pride and, rather than succumb to it we may, when threatened with change, without realizing our motives, instinctively entrench ourselves more firmly in our established position. This, we note, is the third mark given by Durkheim. Possibly we have held to some issue with almost fanatical intensity—which may in itself be an indication that we are suffocating doubts clamouring for expression—and having proclaimed the issue from platform or pulpit, and perhaps written to the papers to support it, it must naturally be a horrific blow to our pride to have to stand before ourselves and others as advocates in another cause. St Paul's experience on the Damascus road is perhaps the most dramatic historical illustration of our meaning. The threat to our loss of self-esteem may, then, often be another factor holding us back from our liberty in Christ.

Yet at this point we need to sound a note of warning. What is usually necessary is to find a middle way, a synthesis between the old and the new. Paul, for all the immensity of his change, saw in his new-found faith the fulfilment and not the rejection of his Jewish background. The moving from one extreme to another will seldom serve the cause of truth, and it is well to recognize this. Thus in the examples we have taken the teetotaller, the Sabbatarian and the fundamentalist will each need to find a balanced position within his new discipline. Further, we may remark that none of what has been said is meant to exclude the holding of firm and deep convictions on the many matters which affect our daily lives, which is a mark of strength and not of weakness. We have used the word 'stubborn' and underlined it, and it is crucial to our inquiry.

And lastly, there is to be a deep and generous charity in this whole area of development, questioning and change. What is less than a mole-hill to one may be a mountain to another. As St Paul tells us, knowledge puffs up, love builds up. And we need a great patience and charity towards ourselves. There has to be an acceptance of our limitations, at least until the Holy Spirit has had time to penetrate to the depths within us. We are not to be surprised if it takes some time for the emotional or feeling side of our nature to correspond with insights we may have perceived with the mind. This child within us may be a long time coming to birth. The acceptance of a position with the mind does not protect us from the painful feelings of guilt—we see it as real, God as morbid, to interpret Julian again—and sometimes many years must pass in preparation for the freedom we may ultimately claim. Surrender and abandonment are the words we want here, that God may do his work in his time and in his way.

Human Nature Restored

Some years ago a lecturer at a summer school in Canterbury began his address by telling of an experiment he had made to find out what, in the minds of people around him, was the greatest enemy of Christianity today. From the first person to whom he addressed his question he received the reply, 'the Roman Catholic Church'. After the laughter had subsided— the lecturer himself being a Roman Catholic—he took us through the catalogue of answers. I cannot recall them all now but I remember there followed a more expected answer— Communism—and I think probably various replies such as apathy, spiritualism, obsession with the occult and so on. Facetious answers were not wanting, though it may be that some of them contained a sting we did not readily detect. And so he went on from one person to the next until he received the answer which satisfied him. The greatest enemy to Christianity today—he had no doubt about it—was Manicheism. Our speaker went on to explain Manicheism as a false division between the material and the spiritual which sees matter and spirit, not as complementary to one another, as does the Christian faith grounded in the incarnation, but as opposed, as acting against one another, the material as evil and the spiritual as good.

Julian would well have understood our lecturer's choice, for she is deeply incarnational, seeing grace always as being for the perfection of our human nature and not for its destruction. It is no accident that the central words in the collect used for Julian's day bear witness to this thought: 'Grant that as we are created in your nature and restored by your grace'[1] —the phrase reaches to the very heart of Julian. For her there is no false division between the material and the spiritual.

She speaks of the glorious union which God has made between the soul and the body, and she writes: 'Our soul together with our body and our body together with our soul. Let either of them take help from the other, until we have grown to full stature.'[2] In this respect Julian was a child of her age, for she lived in times when, as P. F. Chambers writes:

the senses were (seen to be) aids to the spirit and men handled material things as craftsmen of God. The great cathedrals and churches were often a blaze of colour, and their painted walls and coloured windows seemed to be singing, their ceilings appearing like starry skies, or a vision through heaven's opened door. The later reaction and divorce of grace and nature, the severance of the natural from the supernatural, and discontinuity between the human and the divine had not yet clouded the scene. The medieval church was not afraid of the wedding of the material and the spiritual, the soul and the senses in a holy alliance to the glory of God and the inspiration of men.[3]

In such a climate it becomes natural for Julian to write: 'Nature is all good and fair in itself, and grace was sent out to save nature and destroy sin, and bring fair nature back again to the blessed place from which it came, which is God, with more nobility and honour by the powerful operation of grace.'[4] But Julian's most remarkable passage on this aspect of her teaching is not to be found in the English manuscripts of her work at the British Museum, but in the one other extant manuscript deposited at the Bibliothèque Nationale, Paris. It speaks of God's regard for all our human nature right down to its weakest and lowest level. For sheer beauty and delicacy it matches any of the passages of her book:

A man walks upright, and the food in his body is shut in as if in a well-made purse. When the time of his necessity comes, the purse is opened and then shut again, in most seemly fashion. And it is God who does this, as it is shown when he says that he comes down to us in our humblest needs. For he does not despise what he has made, nor does he disdain to serve us in the simplest natural functions of our body, for love of the soul which he created in his likeness. For as the body is clad in the cloth, and the flesh in the skin, and the bones in the flesh, and the heart in the trunk, so are we, soul and body, clad and enclosed in the goodness of God.[5]

It is only the last sentence of our quotation which is to be found in the Sloane manuscripts in the British Museum.

That grace does not destroy nature but perfects it has always been the teaching of the Church. But it is undoubtedly true that the Church, if not through its official teaching, yet through some of its spokesmen, among them some whom it has honoured, and sometimes through its mental and spiritual climate, has often produced another impression: that commonplace things like food and sex and sleep are almost necessary evils, instead of being a part of the means God uses to effect his work of sanctification, to bring us to fullness and completeness in Christ. We cannot do without these things if we and the human race are to survive—people with a Manichaean turn of mind seem to say—but surely God with his vast resources and skills, could he not have thought out a rather better way? Such thinking undermines the Christian faith at its roots. 'Regard the flesh, the body, matter as evil or even inferior, and one has already begun the deviation from Christian truth.'[6]

How different is the teaching and example of Jesus and the New Testament! Jesus accepts the attention of the prostitute in the house of Simon the Pharisee, and turning to his host who has spurned the customary courtesies he replies in answer to his unspoken question:

> I came into your house and you poured no water over my feet, but she has poured out her tears over my feet and wiped them away with her hair. You gave me no kiss but she has been covering my feet with kisses ever since I came in. You did not anoint my head with oil, but she anointed my feet with ointment.[7]

In the matter of food and drink Jesus made himself sufficiently vulnerable to be open to the accusation 'a gluttonous man and a wine-bibber'.[8] He graced a simple wedding ceremony and assisted in its celebrations. He took such sleep as was necessary for him, for although we only read once that he slept, and that was in a boat in a storm, we are told that it was his custom to rise early for prayer, and hence sleep was a part of the normal pattern of his life. And before he died he made provision for his memory to be recalled and his presence to be known through the everyday material elements of bread and wine. Yet all this is but secondary, as it were the accidents of the incarnation. Primarily stands the incarnation itself, God made flesh in the one 'whom we have heard, and have seen with our own eyes, and have watched, and touched with our hands,'[9] God who took upon himself flesh and blood and bones, and all the intricacies and limitations of our human nature.

There may be very good reasons for celibacy, and there may be very good reasons for self-denial in food and drink and the other good things in life. But it would be precarious to attempt to measure standards of goodness and holiness—allowing that each one has his special call from God—by the degree in which these things are present or absent in a man's life. St Paul gives the great principle which in this area is to rule our lives, 'Every creature of God is good, and nothing to be refused if it is received with thanksgiving.'[10] All the good things of life, friendship and marriage, food and drink and sleep, and the many and various pleasures which come to us through our senses, through art, music, nature and so on, are to be—received with thanksgiving—the instruments of our sanctification.

To say this does not mean that at certain stages of our life, or at chosen seasons, there is not to be a reasoned measure of withdrawal, a denial of the senses for a period. That is necessary, but it is important to get the reason theologically right. It is necessary not because the senses are evil, but rather because they are so supremely good that God can never be ultimately satisfied with anything less than their full potential. It is the rhythmic experience of withdrawal and engagement which prevents us from resting and feeding on sense experience, which in fact ultimately blunts our sensibility. Blake has it exactly:

He who bends to himself a Joy
Doth the winged life destroy:
But he who kisses the Joy as it flies
Lives in Eternity's sunrise.

St John of the Cross, who in popular imagination is often
associated only with denial, teaches that we have to be led
from the position in which we rest and feed on sense experience, not (ultimately) to the denial of the joys of sense, but
to a liberty of spirit in the midst of such joys. Any who care
to refer to his teaching[11] will see that he approaches his subject
with a good deal of caution and guards himself carefully from
misinterpretation. But he does go through the senses one by
one and teaches that in God's design all our senses are to be
instrumental in taking us to him. He speaks of beautiful
music, pleasant sights, fragrant smells, delicious tastes, and
soft and delicate touches, and writes that all sense experience
may 'subserve the end for which God created (it), which is
that He should be better loved and known because of (it)'. I
think that the following passage from Julian, although it refers
to life beyond death, illustrates her own evaluation of the part
our senses are to play under God in growth to fullness of life:
'When we die we shall come to God knowing ourselves clearly,
having God wholly. We shall be enfolded in God for ever,
seeing him truly, feeling him fully, hearing him spiritually,
smelling him delectably, and tasting him sweetly.'[12]
In his book *The Roots of a Radical*[13] Bishop John Robinson
remarks on an affinity a part of Julian's writing bears with
Jung in this area of which we have been speaking. He quotes
these words from chapter 56 of the *Revelations:* 'We can never
attain to the full knowledge of God until we have first known
our own soul thoroughly. Until our soul reaches its full development we can never be completely holy; in other words,
not until our sensuality has been raised to the level of our
substance.' I have often thought myself that if Julian were
living today she would find much in Jung to attract her. Take
for example the following passage from the same section as
that above: 'In our Father, God Almighty, we have our being;
in our merciful mother we are remade and restored. Our
fragmented lives are knit together and made perfect man.

And by giving ourselves, through grace, to the Holy Spirit we are made whole.'[14] Or as another translation has it, 'Our separate parts are integrated into perfect man'—overtones of Jung whichever we choose. We are at once reminded of Jung's emphasis on what he terms the principle of individuation, which has been defined as 'the conscious realisation and integration of all the possibilities immanent in the individual'.[15]

Jung stressed that for spiritual and psychological health a man must have a harmonious and friendly relationship with his unconscious. In his encounter with the unconscious there are two opposing extremes, each of which is a danger point. The first danger is, as it were, to let the lid off the unconscious life, to allow the unconscious to surge upwards like an erupting volcano, carrying all before it, flooding the conscious life, overthrowing self-control, leading it may be to loss of mental balance. The other danger occurs when we keep a large part of ourselves locked away in the unconscious, either because we fear what we see, or because we do not like what we see, this dark shadow side of our nature which it is painful for us to reveal even to ourselves. In such a state our life becomes very 'thin', lived without depth at the superficial, conscious level. The emotions are feared, and hence their freedom of flow is inhibited. As we saw in the last chapter, if in the first case the danger was that we should drown, the danger now is that we shall freeze.

Such a man is fragmented, that is to say he is cut off from a large part of himself. Jung taught that if we keep these forces locked away down below two things are going to happen. One is that we shall lose a lot of the energy which might be ours. That is because we are expending psychic energy in holding down forces which might be used in other ways. The second thing that will happen is that we invite the hostility of these forces so that they may turn against us and become dangerous, and emerge in ways harmful to the personality, often at unexpected times and in unwanted places, and sometimes in anti-social ways. The tragedies of which we sometimes read, bringing with them deep humiliation and dismay, may often have their roots, not in a loose and libidinous and uncontrolled life—though that may be the case—but in a strictly repressive life where these unconscious forces have rebelled, and have in the manner of caged animals taken their revenge. In his book *Psychology and Morals*, Professor Hadfield writes, 'The instincts refuse to be regarded as poor relations of which a haughty self is half ashamed. They are partners which give power to the enterprise of our ideals.' He goes on to describe high-browed people, refined, sensitive and intellectual, whose lives may well be marked with perverted idealism, and then in a sentence which bears a strong affinity with Julian he continues: 'It is a paradox that (such) people have to be brought to accept the primitive in their souls, to know that out of the animal may spring the spiritual, to recognise that the human is fashioned not only out of the breath of God, but out of the dust of the earth.'[16]

'Our fragmented lives', writes Julian, 'are (to be) knit together and made perfect man, and by giving and yielding ourselves through grace to the Holy Spirit we are made whole.'

Julian and Prayer: Yearning

Julian's teaching on prayer may be conveniently considered under the three headings: yearning, beseeching and beholding. Although we can trace a process of development here, yearning leading to beseeching, and beseeching to beholding, we must be careful not to suggest that yearning, for example, belongs only to the early stages of the spiritual endeavour, later to be left behind for one of the other two; nor is beseeching a stage which at some later time we outgrow. Such a simplification, as we would expect, would be highly misleading. The three aspects of prayer interpenetrate one another at every point.

Here we may consider yearning, the first of our three words. Although it has a slightly archaic ring, it will be convenient to use it rather than longing as it conveys better the atmosphere of warmth and tenderness which suffuses Julian's writings. Perhaps, too, the word better evokes the element of ardour and intensity in our desire for God.

Yearning is the first mark of the awakened soul and, as we would expect, Julian links it with the crisis of conversion, a process which she describes in chapter 39 of her *Revelations*. Having been chastened by sin, broken and brought near to despair, the Holy Spirit turns bitterness and hopelessness into contrition and hope of God's mercy. As the wounds caused by sin begin to heal, and the soul to revive, the Spirit leads us on to reveal our sins in confession, 'nakedly and truthfully, with great sorrow and great shame' that we have 'so befouled God's fair image'. Julian, apostle of compassion and tenderness, does not shrink from exposing the desolation and havoc which sin wreaks in our lives, nor does she minimize its painful and far-reaching consequences. Bodily sicknesses, sorrows and shames, reproofs and contempts, afflictions and temptations—all these she lists as what we may deservedly expect. But she is quick to add that, accepted humbly as from the hands of God, they become the healing medicines of the soul: and yet more—so great is God's compassion—the scars of sin are seen eventually not as wounds but as honours. It is here in this crisis of conversion that we experience through grace a yearning for God which, with contrition and compassion, lead to deliverance and ultimately to the knowledge of God in the joys of heaven. The reward will be 'great, glorious, and honourable'. 'And so shall all our shame be turned into honour and joy.'

Yet yearning, though associated in a special way with conversion, will always be an element in prayer; indeed its intensity will increase rather than decline with advancing years. The soul which is awakened by the fullness of the joy which is to come must by nature long for its consummation.[1] Julian describes the experience as painful,[2] even as a lasting penance which God mercifully enables us to bear. This suffering, borne in love, must remain until we possess God as our reward.[3] The desert traveller thirsts—if we may use our own image to draw out Julian's thought—for what he has not yet received, and the experience is necessarily painful until he comes to the waters where he may freely drink. Especially will yearning be a mark of the desert times of prayer, empty and dry and seemingly unrewarding. Yearning is here given outward expression in our readiness to persevere. The one who yearns for God is content to sacrifice time and comfort and inclination in waiting for him. To yearning is joined trust,[4] and we are to know in the power of faith—what Julian calls confident trust—that prayer which is dry, savourless and seemingly pointless does good and is pleasing to God.[5]

Not only does yearning for God, in Julian's writing, cover every stage of the Christian life, but the nearer we are to our eternal reward the more intense will it become.[6] It increases with love and never ceases until we see God face to face.[7] We continue to long for God until we die,[8] and with this longing goes rejoicing.[9]

Yet although we have looked at the situation from our side, the deeper truth is that everything proceeds from God. He is the foundation of all that happens, and this our yearning is no exception. It is only in the power of Christ's longing and thirsting for us that we are able to respond.[10] In a notable passage in chapter 59 God is represented as saying, 'I am he who makes you to love. I am he who makes you to long. I am he the endless fulfilling of all true desires.' God's yearning for us opens the way whereby we may come to know him and to love him, and are brought to our eventual reward.

The words we have quoted take us to the underlying truth that our yearning for God does not belong to the realm of nature, as does the desire for food or drink or sleep, but proceeds rather from the order of grace. Yet, as Julian testifies, though planted by God within us, it depends upon our continued co-operation for its development and growth. Alternatively it may die by neglect or be smothered by competing interests. It cannot belong to many to thirst for God on first waking up in the morning, nor on returning home after a busy day. And if the spark within us is to have the chance of burning even as an intermittent flame, there must be times set apart when it is blown upon by the breath of the Spirit. It is the wisdom of the Church to provide for daily Eucharist and Offices, and Julian's own life was, as we shall see, regulated by psalms and prayers to be said at set times through the day. Prayer, she has told us, is the deliberate and persevering action of the soul. It is, thus, not something we fall into naturally, as the eating of our meals, but is an activity begun and sustained by the firm operation of the will. It is only as we embrace a discipline of prayer undergirding life in its rough and difficult patches, and at appointed times taking priority over occupations to which we may be naturally inclined, that we shall know something of the freshness and spontaneity which, as her writings show, Julian herself knew.

Nowhere does Julian speak of the liturgical pattern of prayer which would have marked her life. We can, however, hardly be wrong if we assume that it was based on 'The Ancrene Rule', drawn up for anchoresses a hundred years and more before her time. This was a comprehensive guide covering every aspect of the solitary's life. In relation to prayer it must be remembered that the anchoress of those days often would have been unable to read, and thus matins and evensong and other offices of the Church—and more especially where Latin was required—were often beyond her. Hence the rule made alternative provisions, and it may be that Julian used these whether she was able to follow the regular offices or not. Thus the rule bids the anchoress repeat the Lord's Prayer, the Hail Mary and the Gloria, thirty times in place of matins, twenty in place of evensong and fifteen in place of other offices.[11] In chapter 19 of the Shorter Text Julian gives evidence of her own use of such prayers, 'the Our Father, Hail Mary, I Believe, with such devotion as God will give us'. These devotions would have been repeated again and again, and in some such way, on one occasion at least, Julian spent the whole night, 'and into the morning, until it was a little after sunrise'.[12] This, she tells us, was in a time of special temptation. It is hardly likely, however, that it stood alone.

There was one prayer which was in a very special way to be carried in the heart throughout the day. It bears a striking resemblance to the Jesus Prayer, made familiar to many today through the practice of the Orthodox Church. On rising in the morning, the anchoress was bidden in 'The Ancrene Rule' to say a short form of prayer ending with the words: 'Jesus Christ, Son of the Living God, have mercy on us! Thou who didst condescend to be born of a virgin, have mercy on us!' These words were to be said continuously during the period of dressing and, too, frequently through the day: 'Have these words much in use, and in your mouth, as often as ye may, sitting and standing.'[13]

*

Not everyone is happy—not every Christian is happy—with the idea of repetitive prayer. For many it comes too near to the vain repetitions against which Jesus warns. It is asked whether such prayer is not mechanical, and therefore vain and to no purpose. The question is not without point, but the answer must be that prayer must never become *merely* mechanical. Any activity—and in this respect prayer is the same as any other—if it could ever become *merely* mechanical, would make us robots and not people. So long as another element is always present, and its importance understood, in this case the intention or desire to pray, the mechanical basis on which the words are said is not a matter for concern; nor does it become so when the attention to the words fluctuates again and again as it surely will. The important thing is that the intention to pray remains, ourselves meanwhile attending gently to the words as the Holy Spirit enables us, knowing that the heart is at prayer even though the mind may wander from time to time. We have to remember that the real prayer lies beyond the words in the inclination and the offering of the heart, and the function of the words is to set the heart free to pray. The words may be seen as the banks of a river enabling it to remain deep and flowing. Without the banks the waters would scatter and become shallow and even stagnant. A similar danger is open to prayer when the framework in which it freely flows is removed. Yet the prayer is not the framework but lies beyond. And just as when the river flows into the sea the banks are left behind, so when prayer flows more deeply into God, the words, having served their purpose, will drop away.

The point we are making is admirably illustrated in a fine piece of writing by Maréchal, wherein he speaks of an elderly peasant woman telling her beads before the cottage hearth. The passage is taken from *Worship* by Evelyn Underhill:

> The monotony of these repetitions clothes (her) with physical peace and recollection; and her soul, already directed on high, almost mechanically, by her habitual gesture of drawing out the rosary, immediately opens out with increasing serenity on unlimited perspectives, felt rather than analysed, which converge on God. . . What does it matter then if the (humble soul) does not concern herself with living over and over again the exact meaning of the formula which she is repeating?. . . often she does better, she allows herself to rise freely into a true contemplation, well worn and obscure, uncomplicated, unsystematised, alternating with a return of attention to the words she is muttering, but building up in the long run *on the mechanical basis they afford* a higher, purified, personal prayer.

Evelyn Underhill comments: 'Habit and attention must cooperate in the life of worship. . . Habit alone easily deteriorates into mechanical repetition. . . Attention alone means, in the end, intolerable strain.'[14]

The fact is that what we call repetitive prayer is not strictly speaking repetitive at all. The words, it is true, will be repeated again and again, but it is the total situation with which we are concerned, and that changes from one moment to the next. Seen in this light the tenth blow on a nail is not a repetition of the first because by that time it is nearer its object. So it is that with every repetition of our prayer we are drawn more closely into the knowledge and love of God, and every recitation is made from a different vantage point from the one before. Shirley C. Hughson writes:

> We are not to think that long continuance in the use of the same cry to God means no change. . . . The outward expression may be the same, but the force of no two acts can ever be the same. The fact that five seconds ago I said, 'Jesus, I love Thee', wrought a change in me, so that when I say the same words again, I bring to them a stronger spirit of love and devotion to our Lord than would have been possible in the first instance. The first act brought me into closer and fuller union with Him; and although I may not perceive it, so profound a change was wrought in me that each succeeding act makes upon my character an increasingly powerful impress, the force and effect of which is ever mounting. So, strictly speaking, there is no repetition. It is not the same, but a different thing that is done. Thus, as we go on in the work of prayer, the soul does not, cannot, abide in any one stay. There is a continual deepening of spiritual quality, and intensification of love, and with love all the other virtues flowering every moment into new and richer things.[15]

For the Christian who uses repetitive prayer a eucharistic background is presupposed. Every Eucharist re-presents the whole drama of our redemption—incarnation, cross and passion, resurrection and ascension, and the gift of the Holy Spirit. In it and through it communion is deepened, our lives are nourished, and in the power of the Spirit within the communion of saints we present ourselves again in sacrificial offering. The prayer is to be seen as an extension of the eucharistic offering, and as containing within it, though unexpressed, the theological content of the Eucharist. This need not be a matter for repeated conscious reflection, for if we are people who cherish the Eucharist as being at the heart of our worship, we cannot but bring both its virtue and its content not only into every form of prayer, but into every activity as well.

Whatever form of prayer is chosen, the principles governing its use remain the same. The words are to be repeated again and again with the mind and the heart gently enfolded in them. We have already said that we are not to worry when the mind involuntarily wanders, for the prayer is not lost if the intention remains. At first it will be the mind which is chiefly engaged, but after a time the prayer will descend to the heart and take root within. This is a process which has to be allowed to happen, but we can assist it by mentally looking towards the heart. 'Let the mind descend to the heart' is the advice of the old writers on the Jesus Prayer, and the same applies whatever words may be chosen. It is best to proceed slowly, taking perhaps not more than ten minutes at first once or twice a day. The descent to the heart is not to be expected straightaway, and it may be weeks before we observe this process beginning to take place. From that time the prayer will take root more and more deeply within, and will arise spontaneously from time to time. It will then quite naturally come to share many activities with us.

If a new form of words is chosen, and too much variation is not advisable, it will again take some time, though probably less than before, for the descent to the heart to take place, and longer still for deep lodgement within. Many are aware of this process today through having to discard old patterns of psalmody and liturgical prayer. The words of the old have become the vehicle by which the prayer life within us has for many years been quickened and sustained, building within paths of neural discharge which remain unactivated when a new set of words is given us to recite. This may be necessary for accommodation to a new era, and we have, I believe, to come to terms with it. Moreover, we shall find that the new is not without advantages; but that there are losses as well can hardly be gainsaid.

A lovely likeness has been drawn between the Jesus Prayer and the flight of a bird, it may be that of an eagle. Through the measured beating of her wings, the great bird ascends steadily higher and higher into the upper reaches of the air. Then for a time the wings are spread and still as she glides in graceful flight. After a while, when height has been lost, the motion of the wings begins again. So with our prayer, whatever form it takes, the actual repetition of the words will ebb and flow, and yet, for those practised in it, the prayer will be ever carried in the heart. What matters beyond all is that heart and mind be stayed on God—whether we call this habitual recollection or prayer without ceasing is of no account—and only in so far as it serves that end is repetitive prayer to be cherished and practised.

Although all prayer, whether said alone or in the company of others, is corporate in the sense that it is made within the mystical body of Christ, repetitive prayer of the sort of which we have been speaking does, too, lend itself to corporate use in its more generally understood sense. I recall visiting a church in a small Spanish port, where for an hour before the night-time mass a congregation gathered with their rosaries, repeating their devotions again and again, the group on either side of the central aisle responding to each other. It was a moving experience, and not surprisingly the mass which followed was a truly contemplative activity. This, however, is not a pattern which lends itself lightly to imitation; it grows naturally from the soil, and the earth of Spain is different from our own. But it may well be rewarding for two like-minded people to experiment in this way with the Angelus—perhaps for the music of its words the most lovely prayer ever written—or with the Jesus Prayer. If the latter is used it is said first by one and then the other, a plan which allows for silences as well as words. If three or four are engaged the silences for each are further prolonged. In the case of the Angelus a versicle-response pattern is established. Psalmody may also be used, but it is important that the verses be known by heart. An odd number of verses ensures that neither partner has the same words to repeat each time. The first five verses of Psalm 103 taken from the Book of Common Prayer make an excellent round. Some may think to experiment here.

After a while a passage from the Bible or elsewhere, may be read. A shared silence may be better still. The whole may take about twenty minutes, to be extended to half an hour when both are ready. It may be that experiment on these lines is being widely made. Having worked myself with a friend of like mind I can testify to the value of the experience.

Julian and Prayer: Beseeching

It may come as a surprise to many to learn how much Julian has to say on petitionary prayer. Petition is often regarded as belonging to the lower levels of prayer, something Christians may expect to leave behind as they grow more fully into Christ, and hardly appropriate to the mystical life with which we associate Julian's name. It is therefore worth noting that Julian lays emphasis on this way of prayer, and never does she suggest that we shall outgrow its need. Nowhere is Julian's thought more thoroughly biblical than here. In the Bible the very word prayer, as its etymology strictly demands, is synonymous with petition. Nowadays we commonly use the word to cover every aspect of our communion with God. Confession, colloquy, praise, thanksgiving, worship—these and other words cover one or other facet of the prayer life. Everywhere the Bible witnesses to their importance and commends them to us. But they are not referred to as prayer, which word is kept for petition alone.

The greater part of Julian's direct teaching on prayer is brought to us through her fourteenth revelation and may be found in three central chapters of the longer text of her book.[1] She begins by pointing to two conditions which are to govern the prayer life. Prayer must be 'rightful', and it must be made 'in sure trust'. These rather cryptic terms are expanded in the opening words of chapter 19 of the Shorter Text:

> I saw two conditions in those who pray, according to what I have felt myself. One is that they will not pray for anything at all but for the thing which is God's will and to his glory; another is that they apply themselves always and

with all their might to entreat the thing which is his will and to his glory.

Let us take these conditions in turn. We shall readily agree—every informed Christian will agree—that we may not pray for anything which we have reason to believe to be in conflict with God's will. We engage in prayer not to attempt to bend God's will to ours—which if it were possible would always be to our disadvantage—but in the desire that our will may be brought more closely into line with God's, and that we may be given a clearer conception of what belongs to his glory. Speaking in general terms it is not difficult for us to know what is God's will for ourselves and others. Thus we may always pray for an increase in faith and hope and love, and in this very chapter[2] Julian bids us do so. When, however, we come to particular things, that John may find work, or that Mary may be cured of her sickness, it is often not possible to know whether we are praying in line with God's will or not. Either 'unemployment' or sickness may in certain circumstances provide the spring-board from which God's purposes can best be served, and to wish otherwise for John or Mary may be to do them a disservice. Julian does, however, tell us that we are to pray for particular things, though our prayers here, as at all times, are to be subject to God's will. As an example we may note how she worded one of her own prayers. Julian had long desired that at the age of thirty she might be allowed to share in bodily sight in the Passion of Christ, and that she might suffer bodily sickness seemingly unto death. 'I intended this because I wanted to be purged by God's mercy, and afterwards live more to his glory because of that sickness.'[3] She had also desired to be taken more deeply—she speaks of the experience as 'wounds'—into 'true contrition', 'loving compassion' and the 'longing with my will for God'.[4] She had realized that the first two of her wishes were, to say the least, unusual, and hence when she conceived them—'when I was young', being in some doubt as to whether they were God's will for her, she had framed her prayer in these words: 'Lord, you know what I want, if it be your will that I have it, and if it be not your will, good Lord, do not be displeased, for I want nothing which you do not want.'[5] It may stand as our model in those many cases in which we cannot presume to know God's will. We are to lay our desires plainly and honestly before God, entreating him earnestly, but above all wanting his will to be done; or at least, if this be beyond us, wanting to be brought to want his will.

The second requirement of true prayer is 'confident trust',[6] expanded in the Shorter Text to the applying of ourselves 'always and with all (our) might to entreat the thing which is (God's) will and to his glory'.[7] Thus perseverance is seen as the indication of the reality and depth of our faith. Or seen negatively, if our faith is weak, its weakness will reveal itself in a vacillating and wavering prayer life, perhaps in giving up altogether. Yet this difficulty in trusting is common to us all, and it stems, says Julian, from an uncertainty as to whether God hears our prayers.[8] In turn this doubt has two causes, the first being our sense of unworthiness, the second the absence of feelings in prayer. Remarking that she is drawing on her own experience, Julian writes, 'often we are as barren and dry after our prayers as we were before'. It was on these two points that her fourteenth revelation brought Julian great assurance to counteract her weakness, giving her 'great strength and vitality'.[9] The words given her are among the best known in her book and are basic to her teaching on prayer. In chapter 41 she writes:

> I am the ground of your beseeching. First, it is my will that you should have it, and then I make you to wish it, and then I make you to beseech it. If you beseech it, how could it be that you would not have what you beseech?

We ought, perhaps, to pause here and test our reaction to Julian's teaching. Many well-disposed people who find no problem with, let us say, praise or thanksgiving, find it difficult to come to terms with petitionary prayer. They are likely to tell us that God will surely give what is good whether we pray or not; whereas, if it is bad, a loving God will in any case (it is to be hoped) refuse our request. Would it not, then, be better not to pray, but to leave the issue with God to give or withhold?

The argument looks formidable—even, at first sight, decisive. But let it be transferred for a moment to the world of action, and its flaw—even its absurdity—is at once apparent. Let us suppose that Mother Teresa were to say that she dare not care for the poor of Calcutta because she cannot know whether it is God's will that they shall live or die. If it is his will for one that he shall live, then he will live anyway; if it is his will that he shall die, then she must do nothing to attempt to frustrate that will. Either way it is better to do nothing, but to leave God to work things out as he sees best. Instinctively we know there is something fundamentally wrong in an argument of that sort. We shall at once reply that God's primary concern in the plight of Calcutta's poor is not to be measured in terms of living or dying, but rather in terms of love and caring. If God's design for one is that he shall live, it is never that alone, but that he shall live through the experiencing of another's love and concern, with all the depth and richness that that may bring to each partner in the relationship. If God's design for another is that he shall die, again it is never that alone, but that he shall die in some measure of dignity, and in the knowledge that someone loved and cared. Whatever the outcome, God's design, we may confidently affirm, is that it shall come about through human tenderness and compassion. We cannot stress too strongly that no principle is changed if we now return from the world of action to that of prayer. The manner of application is different, but not the principle itself. As God wills to carry out his designs through our actions, so he wills to forward them through our prayers. If it is God's will that my sick friend shall live it is not that alone, but that he shall live through the prayers of a supporting fellowship, with all that this does to quicken love and deepen relationships. If in God's providence the hour of death is now at hand, it is his will that it shall be passed through supported by the love and care, and strengthened by the faith and hope of the Christian community. The only true death is isolation, and wherever prayer is real, communion or fellowship is being quickened. The argument we first posed has, then, entirely overlooked the fact that God wills to work out his purpose *through* our prayers, with all that that means to the building up of love and trust and hope. Further, by committing any situation to God, our relationship with him is deepened and we are led to see him more clearly and to trust him more surely, as the provider of our needs. 'God appointed prayer', wrote Father Benson of Cowley, 'not because he had any delight in our formal homage but because he desired, by forming in us the habit of prayer, to draw us to himself, the fountain of all good.'[10]

Although Julian does not ask the question we have posed, she repeatedly gives us the answer. The priority is prayer itself, not its effectiveness in terms of tangible results. God wants our prayer and he looks for it. Insistently she presses this point home. In witnessing to its importance Julian even allows herself to say that our prayers will make no difference to what God already intends to do,[11] though in the Longer Text, as though she has gone too far, she omits this observation in a roughly parallel chapter.[12] It seems that what she would have us grasp is that by comparison with her central point, 'results' are quite unimportant. We are to pray and to go on praying, naturally in line with God's will so far as we may discern it. Let that be done, and all is done.

We turn to the text in support of what has been said. In the Shorter Text Julian writes: 'God's love is so great that he regards us as partners in his good work; and so he moves us to pray for what it pleases him to do';[13] and later in the same chapter, 'How could you please me more than by entreating me, earnestly, wisely, sincerely, to do the thing that is my will?' In the Longer Text, chapter 41 speaks of our Lord's great delight in our beseeching, and later Julian writes: 'Our Lord is most glad and joyful because of our prayer; and he expects it, and he wants to have it.'[14] Sometimes it may be that we think that when our prayer is dry and savourless, it is scarcely acceptable to God. Julian assures us that the reverse is the case, for 'in dryness and in barrenness, in sickness and in weakness, then is your prayer most pleasing to me, though you think it almost tasteless to you.' But more strongly still, God 'covets to have us praying continually in his sight', and 'the joy and the bliss that this is to him, and the thanks and honour that we shall have for it, this is beyond the understanding of all creatures in this life.'[15] Most movingly of all, (returning to chapter 41) Julian pictures our prayers as being gathered up by God and stored in a sort of heavenly chest where they will never perish, but stand before God and his saints, 'continually received, always furthering our needs', at the last to be given back to us 'with endless, honourable thanks from him'. It is an affecting picture and invites comparison with the psalmist's words: 'Put thou my tears into thy bottle',[16] our penitential tears being seen as so precious to God that he gathers them up and bottles them in a wine-skin to ensure that not one of them is lost. Poetry, whether here or with Julian, may convey a deeper truth and evoke a fuller response than the more pedestrian language of prose.

This important contribution which Julian makes to the subject of prayer is gathered together with singular clarity and charm in the following passage from her writing:

> Moreover he intends that just as we see him to be doing it, so we should pray for it as well. It is not enough just to do one without the other. For if we pray, not realising that he is already at work, it makes us despondent and sceptical—which is not honouring to him. And if we see him at work yet do not pray, we do less than we ought. May that not happen—and may he not see it so! But to see that he is doing it, and to pray for it at the same time—that honours him, and benefits us. Everything our Lord has ordained to do he wishes us to pray for either specifically or generally. His consequent happiness and joy, and our thanks and glory, pass our power to understand.[17]

God, then, is working out his purpose, and he wants us on our part to see what he is doing, and to pray for it as well. There is no suggestion that our prayers will produce results in the sense of changing the course of events, and as we have seen in the Shorter Text Julian expressly says that prayer makes no difference to what God already intends to do; though we have noted, too, that twenty years later, when she came to write her longer version, she refrains—I suggest deliberately—from reaffirming that view. Even so, she stops short of correcting it, and it seems reasonable to suppose that her considered view is best presented in the words quoted above from chapter 42 of the Longer Text. We may say of that passage that whilst it does not deny that prayer affects the unfolding of events, yet, at the same time, it offers no encouragement that it does.

It may well be that what Julian has written comes to us as an inadequate conception of petitionary prayer when measured against the teaching of the New Testament. I think we may best understand it by presenting her teaching as one aspect of the truth to which we must hold in what must remain in this life the unresolved conflict between determinism and free will. Looked at from God's side, his plan is known from all eternity and will move forward inexorably to its appointed end. But seen in this way God's vision must encompass everything, and so our prayers themselves are a part of it. We may illustrate this idea with an incident from St John's Gospel, where Jesus and his disciples encounter a man who was blind from birth. The New English Bible brings out the meaning sharply: 'His disciples put the question, "Rabbi, who sinned, this man or his parents? Why was he born blind?" "It is not that this man or his parents sinned," Jesus answered; "he was born blind that God's power might be displayed in curing him." '[18] Thus, Jesus sees the *total* sequence of events as proceeding from the hands of God. Everything is caught up in God's action, the blindness from birth, the prayer or the opportunity to heal, the subsequent life of the man healed. Dom Aelred Graham has some powerful words we may ponder here: 'Are we to infer that the eternal plan in God's mind has been in some way altered in consequence of a creature's prayer? . . . Far from changing God's designs our prayers are the instrument from all eternity by which he has decreed to carry them out.'[19] As we grow in the Christian life, this is likely to be increasingly the vantage point from which we view our question. It is only as we would expect that Julian herself would so see it.

This is not the only approach, however, and we must try to do justice to both sides. It is, moreover, important that we should do so. Where, we may ask, is the incentive to pray if we do not believe our prayer can have some part in the modification of events? Would the early Church have prayed for the release of Peter from prison unless it had believed that prayer might in some way be instrumental in bringing it about?[20] That may stand for the hundreds of cases we might quote from the Bible, or history, or our own experience. If Aelred Graham has a truth we do well to hold in mind in the above quotation, so does Ronald Knox in this extract from a sermon on prayer:

> God, in his wisdom, has annexed some of his blessings, we do not know in what manner or measure, to our patience and confidence in asking for them. . . . Ask and you shall receive; he doesn't want us to puzzle our heads over the machinery of it all, he wants us to go to him like children, not ashamed to tell him what we have set our hearts on. Only, at the back of it all, the object of prayer is not to make God want what we want, it is to make us want what God wants. . . . In his will lies our peace.[21]

That God has linked some of his blessings to our patience and confidence in asking for them is a truth every Christian must surely affirm. If it be not possible to reconcile it with what has been said earlier, that does not mean we are to ignore it. It means, rather, as so often happens, that we are to hold together two seemingly conflicting truths in creative tension, and move forward as best we can.

Looking now at prayer from this second point of view, it will be helpful if we regard it, not for the changing of God's will, which even if it were possible we would not wish to bring about, but rather for its releasing. A father may desire to send his son for higher education. The boy shows little inclination at school to work, and it seems that less ambitious plans should be made. The time comes, however, when he begins to take his studies seriously, enabling the father's will to be released to do what he had all along wanted to do.

Taking that example over into the region of prayer we may imagine parents pleading with God for the life of their seemingly dying child. If we suppose them to be selfish and possessive then to grant their request may be to hand the boy over to a living death. But if a time comes when with all the energies of the soul these same parents can pray the God-united loving prayer, 'Your will be done', is it not clear they have become ready (if God so wills) to receive the child from God's hands into a relationship in which the boy's life will thrive—and theirs too? And if we are looking at prayer from this angle, we may say this is the moment God must be looking for and waiting for. Thus his action which in the name of love was previously withheld can now in the name of love be released. What would have been before for the child's hurt now becomes for his good. This is just one example of a principle which runs through the intercessory life. We have to grasp that it is our selfishness which so often stands in the way of the blessings which God longs to bestow.

I have offered two lines of thought, but we have to acknowledge that it is impossible to reconcile them from our present standpoint. For God, time—if we may use the word at all—is an eternal now, whereas for us it is a succession of present moments. I believe that Julian might well have said in an idiom made familar in an earlier chapter that in God's eyes everything is foreknown, in our eyes it is open to modification and change; that both are true, but that God's insight is the deeper one. We may hold, as does Julian, to the deeper insight, but it is a leap of faith, and our finite minds cannot penetrate the mystery. There we must leave it, content to be caught up in the paradox of God's foreknowledge (a gentler and better word than determinism) and man's free will, which admits of no resolution, at least this side of eternity.

Yet, although we cannot resolve the problem which lies behind intercessory prayer, we can with profit reflect that it remains a practical problem for us only in so far as we live in a partially converted state. Recently I was privileged to be shown a letter written by a young mother to a Sister of a religious community. It was one of the most courageous letters I have ever read.

The Lord has given us a beautiful baby daughter. Her name is Rachel and she was born on Monday the 15th of June at 3 a.m. weighing 6lbs 3oz. She has spina bifida and hydrocephalus (fluid on the brain), both of which are too bad for the doctors to do anything and they only expect her to live for a few weeks. But we know that God is in control of the situation and he has given us great peace in our hearts. We look to Him for his will to be done in her life. We both came out of hospital two weeks ago and John and I are both thoroughly enjoying having her at home.

We live a day at a time and thank the Lord for each 24 hours with her. She eats and sleeps well—most nights she goes 8–10 hours between feeds. I do hope you are both keeping well. Thank you again for looking after us so well over Easter. We do feel that the Lord really used that time to prepare us for the birth of Rachel. How good he is! Do join us in praising God for the gift of little Rachel and for a safe delivery. Love.[22]

We may well wonder at the faith and courage which lies behind a letter such as this. Quoted in full it reveals the intense human delight shared by these two in the presence of their little daughter. And yet everything is so fully surrendered into the hands of God that whatever the outcome it will become the occasion for praise and thanksgiving. It is this which is its purpose for us at this point. Once we have so deeply entered into the heart and purpose of God, that we can, as St Paul bids us, give thanks whatever happens,[23] the problem of intercessory prayer is not so much resolved as raised to a level where it ceases to arise.

Julian never explores prayer from the second angle we have taken in this chapter. But she does repeatedly insist that we pray for the priorities—mercy and grace, forgiveness, faith and hope and love. There can be no problem here, for these are gifts God always wills to give us. And Julian enters a protest against our storming God with special requests, as though we would pressurize him to give the outcome we desire to some difficult situation.[24] But we may close by letting her speak for herself, and her words will provide the setting for the next chapter:

Then the way we often pray came into my mind and how, through lack of knowing and understanding of the ways of love, we pester him with petitions. . . Then I saw truly that it gives more praise to God and more delight, if we pray steadfast in love, trusting his goodness, clinging to him by grace, than if we ask for everything our thoughts can name. . . All our petitions fall short of God and are too small to be worthy of him, and his goodness encompasses all that we can think to ask. . . The best prayer is to rest in the goodness of God knowing that that goodness can reach right down to our lowest depths of need.[25]

9

Julian and Prayer: Beholding

We began our last chapter by noting the emphasis Julian places on petition when she comes to speak of the life of prayer. We said that to many her emphasis may come as a surprise. To some it may be a disappointment, for beseeching—to return to Julian's word—as often encountered, may not be experienced as a rewarding way of prayer. It may, for example, be presented in a manner which will stretch the mind, or play on the emotions, but do little to engage the heart and will. The contemplative element is missing, or at least the style of presentation does not easily lead us into this way of prayer. But petition, with Julian, has within it, as will already have been evident, a marked element of contemplation and is sometimes indistinguishable from contemplative prayer. Thus Julian writes: 'Beseeching is a true and gracious, enduring will of the soul, united and joined to our Lord's will by the sweet, secret operation of the Holy Spirit.'[1] Words such as these are more nearly descriptive of contemplative than of petitionary prayer. It will, therefore, be helpful to coin a word to describe beseeching or prayer as we now meet it, and I propose to use the compound word 'contemplative-petition'.

To one who is called to the contemplative life, every form of prayer offered by the Church becomes the occasion for contemplative-petition. It will be found through the Daily Office, or yet more in the eucharistic rite which is a mosaic of petition, praise, thanksgiving and other elements supporting one another in delicate balance. Or we shall encounter it in what some have called the Little Office, in the reciting of the Jesus Prayer or the Hail Mary, or in the repeating of collects and psalms and the like. All such petitionary prayer, through the action of the Holy Spirit, may be, and for those who use it regularly almost certainly will be, a contemplative activity. If we may take two familiar Julian phrases, the first of which we have already noted, it is a way of prayer which 'oneth the soul to God'[2] or makes the soul 'of one accord with God'.[3]

It will be clear that we are now considering petition in a wider setting from that generally considered in the last chapter. The word is so often associated with asking God for tangible things like world peace, or recovery from sickness, or money for missions, that we sometimes overlook the petitionary nature of our commonest prayers. Thus it would probably come as a surprise to most people to learn that in Psalm 119 alone there are approximately seventy petitions. When Julian speaks of prayer or beseeching, she is for by far the most part understanding it at this fundamental level. 'I am yours, O save me', 'O God, make speed to save us', 'O send out your light and your truth that they may lead me'—it is prayers of this sort which are representative of Julian's 'beseeching'. Such entreaties, in their setting of praise and adoration as we meet them in the psalms, are for us, as they would have been for Julian, an extension to the basic prayers she gives—'the Our Father, Hail Mary, I Believe'[4]—and said 'with such devotion as God will give us', they are to be offered on behalf of 'all our fellow Christians, and for every kind of person as God wishes'. They thus become prayers of intention for whatever cause we have in mind, and it is likely to be in this way that most people will come to the experiencing of intercession as a contemplative activity. Here then is another understanding of what we mean by contemplative-petition.

We are not, however, to confine contemplative-petition to vocalized prayers. Our hearts and minds are drawn into prayer through our actions as well as through our lips. This step takes us beyond anything Julian has written, but with the wealth of ritual which marked the Church of her day it would have been understood in her generation better than in ours. Familiar symbolic acts such as lighting a candle, censing the altar or turning the page of the Roll of Honour have within them elements both contemplative and petitionary. So too contemplative silence before God is not without its petitionary element, and for many, used with intention for the needs laid upon them, this will be their main expression of intercessory prayer. We may, of course, go further and say there is no activity—or suffering—which cannot be offered with petitionary intent. Washing up, or walking down the street, or being patient with someone who bores you can be as truly petitionary as verbalized prayer. More austere practices such as almsgiving or fasting fall into the same category when lovingly and gladly offered. Indeed, in God's design our lives are to become, in Origen's famous phrase 'one great unbroken prayer'.

Although Julian speaks extensively of beseeching in her three central chapters on prayer,[5] there will come a time, she tells us, when it will be left behind. Beseeching is then swallowed up in beholding.

> We pray to him urgently that he may do what is pleasing to him, as if he were to say: How could you please me more than by entreating me, urgently, wisely and sincerely, to do the thing that I want to have done? And so the soul by prayer is made of one accord with God.
>
> But when our courteous Lord of his special grace shows himself to our soul, we have what we desire, and then for that time we do not see what more we should pray for, but all our intention and all our powers are wholly directed to contemplating him. And as I see it, this is an exalted and imperceptible prayer; for the whole reason why we pray is to be united into the vision and contemplation of him to whom we pray, wonderfully rejoicing with reverent fear, and with so much sweetness and delight in him that we cannot pray at all except as he moves us at the time.[6]

Julian knew two types of contemplation of which the first, which may be called the beholding of direct vision, is described here. It seems that she experienced it extensively, and she tells us that at such times there is an inner compulsion which holds the soul to the contemplation of its object. Thus: 'We can do no more than contemplate him and rejoice, with a great and compelling desire to be wholly united into him, and attend to his motion and rejoice in his love and delight in his goodness.'[7] Julian reveals her own experiences in a number of places, perhaps never more movingly than in chapter 14 of the Longer Text, where 'her mind being lifted up to heaven', she saw

> our Lord as a lord in his own house where he had called his much-loved friends and servants to a banquet. . . Completely relaxed and courteous, he was himself the happiness and peace of his dear friends, his beautiful face radiating measureless love like a marvellous symphony; and it was that wonderful face shining with the beauty of God that filled that heavenly place with joy and light.[8]

Writing in chapter 68 of a not dissimilar experience, Julian comments: 'The soul is wholly occupied by the blessed divinity, sovereign power, sovereign wisdom, and sovereign goodness.' Once again, then, she witnesses to the compelling nature of such an experience where the soul is caught up in the vision and must needs attend. Scriptural analogies may be found in the experience of the disciples at the transfiguration,[9] when—we may presume—they could not but gaze on the glory revealed; or in the experience of St Paul caught up into the third heaven.[10]

It must be that only a very few are likely to approach anything of a similar intensity, and yet probably most awakened people can point to one or two incidents which will bear a faint comparison. They have, perhaps, experienced an ecstatic awareness, not necessarily in a religious context as generally understood, but perhaps in the presence of great art or music, or simply coming upon them unexpectedly when they could point to no immediate cause. Thus I may say that in a case to my knowledge—and I suspect it is fairly typical—a person has known three such occasions, one at the age of eleven when travelling alone by train, one as a young man when lying awake in bed at three in the morning, and the third at the altar-rails in the laying on of hands. William Wordsworth, whose heart 'dances with the daffodils',[11] may stand for many who have shared the same transcendence through nature. Julian experienced her 'shewings' often at the time of prayer—'when our . . . Lord shows himself . . . we do not see what more we should pray for. . .'[12]—and it has been the same in the lives of many of the saints.

We have no means of knowing how often the beseeching of which Julian speaks led on to the experience of direct vision. But we can hardly be wrong in thinking that its outcome was more generally a loving attention to God in the obscurity of faith, as the teaching of the Church would have led her to expect. Certainly we shall expect that for ourselves, and it would be presumptuous to look for anything beyond. If, sometimes, more is given—'a shaft of spiritual light which pierces (the) cloud of unknowing'[13]—there may be a variety of reasons, not least a concession to our weakness, a support to our flagging faith. Julian saw her own 'shewings' to be, at least in part, for the strengthening of her fellow-Christians.

In all this I was greatly moved in love towards my fellow Christians, that they might all see and know the same as I saw, for I wished it to be a comfort to them, for all this vision was shown for all men. . . . Everything that I say about me I mean to apply to all my fellow Christians, for I am taught that this is what our Lord intends in this spiritual revelation. And therefore I pray you all for God's sake, and I counsel you for your own profit, that you disregard the wretch to whom it was shown, and that mightily, wisely, and meekly you contemplate upon God, who out of his courteous love and his endless goodness was willing to show it generally, to the comfort of us all. For it is God's will that you accept it with great joy and delight as if Jesus had shown it to you.[14]

I am not good because of the revelations, but only if I love God better, and inasmuch as you love God better it is more to you than to me. I do not say this to those who are wise, because they know it well. But I say it to you who are simple, to give you comfort and strength; for we are all one in love, for truly it was not revealed to me that God loves me better than the humblest soul who is in a state of grace. For I am sure there are many who never had revelations or visions, but only the common teaching of Holy Church, who love God better than I. If I pay attention to myself I am nothing at all, but in general I am, I hope, in the unity of love with all my fellow-Christians. For it is in this unity that the life of all men consists who will be saved.[15]

*

It is likely that for many people the Daily Office will be a way in to a simple form of contemplative prayer, in which reasoning and imagination are hushed and the soul is stayed on God. Equally it may be what we have earlier called the Little Office which may, indeed, be so 'little' as to come down to a single collect or phrase. Remembering the sort of entreaties which Julian for the most part had in mind when she speaks of petition, it was probably for her too psalmody or repetitive prayer of one sort or another through which she was prepared for contemplation, whether for the 'exalted and imperceptible' prayer of which she speaks, or the more simple loving attention to God sustained by a steady though almost unperceivable activity of the will. Especially did she find the need of vocal prayer when 'the heart is dry and feels nothing',[16] or when suffering 'the temptation of our enemy', saying that at such times 'reason and grace drive the soul to implore our Lord with words recounting his blessed Passion and great goodness'. 'O Saviour of the world, who by thy cross and precious blood hast redeemed us: save us and help us, we humbly beseech thee, O Lord.' Julian's Little Office may well have taken on such words as these.

Some years ago, when I lived within the pleasant surroundings of a religious community, I sought to describe the movement of 'beseeching' to 'beholding' through the way of the Office—equally it may be of the Little Office—employing an illustration made real at that time:

The words of the office become the framework of our prayer and are there to support us when we need them. As I looked out of my window the other day, I watched a large and—it seemed to me—rather old pheasant on the lawn. It ran along the grass, took a short flight, and then, being tired, returned to earth once more. There followed a little more running, another flight and return, and so on. It occurred to me that that can be rather like the saying of the office. We move 'with such devotion as God gives us' from one verse to the next in the psalms, and then there may be, as it were, a short period on the wing, when the words, though still recited, recede into the background, and somehow we are taken beyond them, and held for a few moments in that stillness which is God. And then—and this too is our point—just as our pheasant had the good solid earth to return to and support him as he moved forward again, so we have the words of the office to return to and be our support. The bird could not just fall into a void, and in the same way the words of the office prevent us from falling back into the distracting and discordant imagery which often holds our minds. Thus the office may be a way in to contemplative prayer, little bursts of it as the bird made little bursts of flight. But before it does this for us, the repetition of the words with due attention as the Spirit empowers us can be a tremendous help in enabling us to collect our minds, and leave behind the concerns and perplexities of life which so often scatter our mental and spiritual energy.[17]

In the traditional teaching of the Church contemplative prayer is divided into two stages. In the first, known as acquired contemplation, the emphasis is upon my own efforts, aided—as always—by grace. The second stage, known as infused contemplation, is the gift of God. I can do nothing to determine it, though diligent application in acquired contemplation will help to dispose me to receive it. None the less, we must stress, it is of God's free gift when it comes, and there is thus a definite break between the acquired and the infused. It is as though a man rows a boat out into the sea, everything at this stage depending upon him; though we do not forget that in the last resort God gives him the strength to row. A breeze springs up, and he draws in the oars, and from now onwards sails before the wind. The point of the illustration is that he can never determine the moment at which the wind arises, nor its strength when it comes, and no extra working on the oars will serve to hasten it or to change its force. There may be days when he has to row the whole way, and other days when the wind is there to greet him when he goes down to the shore. A further point we may take is that even under sail the man is not idle. Although his work is less perceptible than before, he still has to set the sails and direct the boat. We cannot press the details too far, but in infused contemplation there remains a steady application of the intellect and the will. The operation of the intellect, however, is now so much simplified, its discursive activity having virtually ceased, that it will be almost imperceptible, or entirely so, to the one who prays.

There are some, however, who would find the above illustration too artificial. They would wish to eliminate the sharp division between the rowing and the sailing. For them it will always be a matter of more or less. It is as though a man steadily pours wine into a jug containing a little water, the mixture growing richer all the time, there being no moment when one stage ceases and another begins. So, they would say, the Holy Spirit acts upon us in the same way from the very beginning of prayer, which becomes increasingly passive, or resembling the state of infused contemplation, as the Spirit becomes more and more the dominant partner.

There is a contradiction between these views, and rather than attempting to reconcile them it is better to see them as supplementing one another. We have the same antithesis in the teaching of Jesus: 'Ask, and it shall be given you; seek, and you shall find.'[18] In asking for something I am dependent upon the generosity and good will of another, whereas in seeking my success depends upon the thoroughness and enterprise of my search. Either illustration comes to the aid of the other. We may note, however, that Jesus adds a third: 'Knock, and it shall be opened to you', a reminder that in the last resort truly everything depends on God.

We can never separate our own activity in prayer from the work of the Holy Spirit within us, unless it be simply for the purpose of analysis. In practice the two work together all the time. As well ask whether the student learns because he listens, or because the teacher speaks. We can endlessly discuss the importance of either, but if learning is to take place there must be a continual blending of the two. We have the same dichotomy in the Eucharist, where some stress the gift of God and others the faith which receives it. But sound Christian doctrine insists that although the psychological and spiritual needs of a person at any particular stage may make one aspect for him or her more important than the other, the two must be held together all the time, and we may never lose sight of either. A meal with no digestion to assimilate it is as useless as a digestion with no meal to feed it. Taking them together we may hope to go from strength to strength.

Julian, to whom we may now return, comes down firmly on the side of the Church in its traditional teaching of acquired and infused contemplation.[19] Rather confusingly for our present purpose she uses the word 'seeking'—quite legitimately—with a different shade of meaning to that which we have adopted here. Both the yearning and the beseeching of the Longer Text are covered by the word 'seeking', which 'pleases God greatly. For (the soul) cannot do more than seek, suffer, and trust. And this is accomplished in every soul, to whom it is given by the Holy Spirit.'[20] This stage belongs to all Christians: 'Seeking is common to all, and every soul can have (it) through grace and ought to have (it).' But then comes something which is beyond our power in the way of grace to initiate or hasten or achieve. The corollary to seeking is finding, and in the same chapter Julian writes: 'An illumination by finding is of the Spirit's special grace, when it is his will.' Such finding is full of refreshment and delight: 'Seeking with faith, hope and love pleases our Lord, and finding pleases the soul and fills it full of joy.' But she is quick to add that 'seeking is as good as contemplating, during the time that he wishes to permit the soul to be in labour'. And finally she exhorts us that 'it is God's will that we seek on until we see him, for it is through this that he will show himself to us, of his special grace, when it is his will'.

'That we seek on until we see him.' What is this 'seeing' of which Julian speaks, and to whom is it given? It appears that Julian regards it as being reserved not for a few elect persons, but rather for all called to the contemplative life ready to 'seek, suffer and trust', if and when God wills. Yet Julian could certainly not have expected that those who read her pages would experience 'shewings' as vivid and dramatic as her own, which we may safely say are given to very few. Even so, the quotations taken from her writings in the foregoing paragraph can only mean that Julian encourages us to believe that those who respond generously and wholeheartedly to the contemplative call may expect on occasions—'when it is his will'— to be granted an experience similar in kind, if not in degree, to those which she herself knew. Our 'seeing' may perhaps be aptly called 'a little shewing'. We have referred earlier to the 'shaft of spiritual light' which may break into our prayers, spoken of in *The Cloud of Unknowing*. It may be we are to see it rather as a lighthouse beacon bursting for a few moments through the darkness of a foggy night, to cheer and encourage the mariner on his way and confirm that he is yet on course. *The Cloud* also speaks in the same chapter of a 'stirring of God's love', an experience which makes the work of prayer 'full restful and full light . . . that before was full hard'.[21] It is, I think, on some such lines as these that we are to look for understanding. Our thought may lead us on to a consideration of *The Cloud*, where we shall, for the time being, leave Julian largely behind, to return to her again in our final chapter.

The Greatest Revelation is Stillness

It may come as a disappointment to some readers that no-where does Julian give an account of the method of her contemplative prayer. This is in marked contrast to another book of her time, which in our day has become a classical guide in the way of contemplation. *The Cloud of Unknowing* may not have been written when Julian wrote her *Revelations* in about 1393, though some authorities place its writing one or two decades earlier. At any rate it seems unlikely that Julian had read it when she wrote her book though she may, of course, have come to know it later. There are, however, references in the *Revelations* which suggest that Julian's way was similar to that of *The Cloud*, though quite apart from them it would be reasonable to assume that that was so.

In chapter 18 of the Longer Text Julian refers to St Denis of France. She is not speaking of him in regard to prayer, and we can make no conclusive deduction from her reference. But it does seem strange that he should be sufficiently present to her mind to receive mention at all. This Denis was in Julian's day thought to be Dionysius the Areopagite, who in turn was regarded as the writer of several works on which *The Cloud* was based. Dionysius was a convert of St Paul at Athens,[1] mentioned just once in the New Testament and then lost to history. We now know that Denis of France lived a century and more later than the Areopagite though, as we have said, that was not known to Julian, who thought the two persons to be one and the same. The point is that Julian's reference to Denis, whom she took to be Dionysius, himself an almost unknown New Testament figure, inevitably suggests that she may have had another reason to be interested in him, namely her practice in the Dionysian way of prayer. But here, too, is

a further confusion. Although the writer of *The Cloud* thought
that the source-books of his own inspiration went right back
to the New Testament, that is to books written by Dionysius
the Areopagite in the first or early second century, we now
know that *The Cloud*'s author was drawing on writings from
the early sixth century, composed by a writer whose name is
not known, but who published his work in the name of the
New Testament Dionysius to give it greater authority. This
was a literary device not uncommon in earlier times, and
New Testament students are well acquainted with it. It was
not until several centuries after Julian that it was established
that the books said to be written by the Areopagite were in
fact written in the sixth century. The unknown writer is
usually known as pseudo-Dionysius.

There is no need for the reader to master the details of the
foregoing paragraph. Our purpose is simply to draw attention
to the likely link between Julian and the pseudo-Dionysian
way of prayer, pointing in the direction of a common source
which was the inheritance of both Julian and the author of
The Cloud.

Our argument, however, finds further support in the comparison of the following passages. The left-hand column is
taken from chapter 8 of *The Epistle of Privy Counsel*, written by
the author of *The Cloud* and firmly pseudo-Dionysian in
thought. The other column is taken from chapter 5 of the
Revelations.[2]

... strip, spoil and utterly unclothe thyself of all manner of feeling of thyself, that thou mayest be able to be clothed with the gracious feeling of God himself. And this is the true condition of a perfect lover, only and utterly to spoil himself for that thing that he loveth, and not admit nor suffer to be clothed but only in that thing that he loveth.

He is our clothing that, for love, wrappeth us up and windeth us about ... We need to have knowledge of this—that we should reckon as naught everything that is made, to love and have God who is unmade ... When the soul is willingly naughted, for love, so as to have him who is all, then is she able to receive ghostly rest.

Taking, then, the view that Julian's way of contemplative prayer bore a marked affinity to the way of *The Cloud* and its successor *Privy Counsel*, which marks a maturing of the author's thought, it will be appropriate to look to these two books for the information we are now seeking.

In contrast to the *Revelations, The Cloud*—as we have noted—has much to say about method in prayer. Later we shall speak of this in some detail, but first it will be well to sound a note of warning. We come to God by love and not by navigation,[3] and not even the best charts can of themselves take us to the harbour where we would be. It is hardly necessary to say that the author of *The Cloud* is well alive to this. The 'sharp dart of longing love',[4] or some equivalent phrase, is an important and recurring feature of his works, and his well-known words of the same chapter (reverting to the early form), 'By love he may be gotten and holden, by thought never', underlie all that he has written. So, too, he is at pains to emphasize the theological background of the prayer life, and how all that we do—no matter how hard we may work—is in vain apart from what God has already done in Christ.

All men, who by their good works done according to their lights show they want to be saved, can only be saved now and hereafter by the Passion of Christ, who offered himself as the true sacrifice. His sacrifice was made for all men in general, and not for some individuals in particular. . . . So he, truly and perfectly sacrificing himself for the good of all, does all that is possible to him to unite men with God as effectively as he himself is united to him.[5]

These are foundation thoughts, and they undergird all that we say as we move on to speak of the place of method or technique in prayer.

Technique is a necessary and important factor in everything we do. We need it to play the piano, cook the lunch, or simply to walk down the street. We are not to belittle it, much less to despise it, but we are to remember that it holds always a subordinate position; that is to say, technique is instrumental to an end, but is not to be confused with the end itself. In prayer the end is encounter, fellowship, communion with God within the Body of Christ, and so long as technique remains subordinate to that end it may be learned and welcomed. Very considerably in prayer, but by no means exclusively, technique has to do with the body. 'Our soul together with our body and our body together with our soul. Let either of them take help from the other,'[6] writes Julian, and although she was not at that moment considering the prayer life, its application to prayer would have been self-evident. In the end, however, technique in prayer, as in every other occupation, is likely to become so much second nature that we shall employ it without ordinarily being aware of it; or there may come a time when it will be transcended, rather as for an experienced writer the rules of grammar may be transcended, giving him a freedom of expression which no O-level examiner would allow.

Strangely, perhaps, *The Cloud* has very little to say about the body at prayer, though a good deal to say about the application of the mind and the will. Nowadays in most books the balance is restored, or it may be that the scales are tipped in the direction of the body. Our new awareness is clearly in large part due to the closer contact we have with Eastern faiths, and we owe a debt to the East for impressing the importance of the body, which has been too often overlooked. It is true that in monastic houses, kneeling upright or sitting upright or standing is seen as part of the discipline of prayer and office, and facilities for correct sitting or kneeling are usually designed accordingly. The same, unfortunately, cannot be said of many of our churches.

Before we pass on to *The Cloud*, which, as we have noted, says little about the body at prayer—though what it does say, as we shall see, is extremely interesting—let us look at the question as we may present it today. I was put through my own paces in India by a Roman Catholic priest who himself had been trained in the Hindu tradition. He would act as a true Eastern Guru, watching his pupils as they sat before him, correcting them if they grew careless or slack. He was, himself, an extremely supple person, and in his own meditation most at home in the full lotus posture, a position which few could adopt without extensive training. However, he only asked of his pupils such postures as they could maintain with some measure of ease. The point he was concerned to stress was that whatever the posture taken, the back was to be straight. This is not to say that it was to be ramrod straight, but rather that it should be held in a firm and easy tension allowing for the natural curvature of the spine. Thus there were a number of possible positions: standing, sitting on an upright chair, kneeling upright, kneeling down and sitting on one's heels or on a prayer stool placed so as to bridge the calves, or cross-legged on the ground in the half or full lotus posture, with feet tucked into the body as well as may be. The head was to be held firmly on the neck and to be level, that is to say the neck not bent backwards or forwards. The shoulders were to be kept down, a point needing checking from time to time.

The easy tension in the back was to be balanced by a counter-relaxation at the forehead and temples. The importance of the eyes was frequently stressed. There were six sets of muscles related to the eyeballs, and they were all to be allowed to relax. With the eyes closed we were to look mentally to the middle of the chest at the level of the heart. 'Let your eyeballs feel as if they are dropping out.' The muscles of the face and those around the nostrils were to be relaxed, and the mouth was to be lightly closed, thus allowing for breathing through the nose. So we were to sit in complete stillness for twenty minutes or up to half an hour, looking mentally to the chest and allowing our thoughts to drop away. If the posture is held rightly, the back will be curved in slightly at waist level. This releases the belly, which in turn brings the diaphragm down, thus deepening the breathing.

Breathing was important. At the start we were to take two or three deep breaths to break up the breathing pattern. After that we were to let the breath come and go as it would. Sometimes we were told to put our minds into our breathing, that is to say, mentally to watch and follow the breathing process. We were often reminded that few people breathe properly, the breath being too shallow, engaging almost only the upper part of the lungs. It is difficult to communicate on paper what we were taught. But if anyone cares to lie flat on his back on the floor, with knees bent and near to the floor, with legs crossed and feet drawn up unstrainedly towards the trunk, he will find himself in a position in which he will naturally breathe correctly. By observing the bodily motions, the belly rising first (giving a wave-like motion), it will not be difficult to extend the practice to other positions. Once one has got into the way of things, it is best to forget the breathing and let it take care of itself.

After twenty minutes or so in the meditation position, we were instructed to lie flat on our backs on the floor. Eyes might be open or lightly closed, tensions were to be allowed to drop away. The legs were to be slightly apart, and the arms a little way out from the sides. The hands were to be open, resting on the floor, preferably with the palms upwards. If in this position the thumbs fell naturally to the floor—no forcing—that indicated that the relaxation was good. The 'corpse' posture was to be held in complete stillness for another twenty minutes. If one went off to sleep, as sometimes happened, that was not good in terms of what one was meant to be doing, though in terms of sleep it was excellent, more refreshing and invigorating than the sleep one might expect to get at night. Here again in the corpse posture the ever-active mind, likened in Indian thought to the monkey leaping from branch to branch, would want to busy itself with ideas suggested by memory or imagination. These thoughts are not to be encouraged, but if they present themselves of their own accord they are not to be directly opposed. It may take courage to suffer what presents itself from the unconscious at such times. The thoughts though noticed (inevitably) should not be attended to, developed or followed, but simply allowed to pass by and in the end to float away. One way is to return the attention gently to the body, giving whispered instructions to the arms or some other part—this can be done silently—to release their tension. All thinking creates tension, not in itself bad, but it is not what is wanted at this time. But one has to speak gently to the body, which responds to coaxing but reacts adversely to a sharp command. As the relaxation deepens there will be an increase in blood flow to the skin and we shall feel warmer. It will also seem to us that we are growing heavier and sinking into the ground. Both these features are evidence of a good measure of relaxation.

The state we are now in may best be described as relaxed awareness or passive attention. Psychologically it may be

compared to that of someone standing passively but atten-
tively before a great work of art, not with a view to criticism,
but simply to allow its beauty to be absorbed. We need to
note that relaxation is quite different from what we usually
understand when we say that a person is doing nothing. The
corpse posture needs as much resolution to maintain steadily
as do those we more normally associate with prayer. Relaxation has been described as an attention to the reality of the
present moment. In the end it has to be allowed to happen,
though there are things we can do to help it happen. Incidentally, let it be said in passing that if anyone suffering from
insomnia practises the corpse posture for ten minutes each
night on going to bed, it may not be long before sleeping
tablets can be dispensed with. A firm bed is, however, essential; otherwise, as one teacher of relaxation puts it, the bed
relaxes and not you. Pillows should not be used, but if one
pillow does seem to be necessary it should be pulled well
down towards (not under) the shoulders so as to support the
neck. Relaxation practised last thing at night can well be
linked consciously, though very simply, with prayer. Words
such as 'Into your hands I commend my spirit' give suitable
expression to our intention at such times. Intruding thoughts
can be quietly surrendered into God's hands to be taken care
of while we sleep. After ten minutes or so the pillows can be
adjusted, and we can turn to our normal sleeping position.

But to return. How are we to apply our teaching in a
western setting? People do not take lightly to unfamiliar ways,
though the young are perhaps more adventurous. Two days
ago, as I write this, five young people came for instruction in
the Julian Cell. We finished with a period of silence which I
think was a revelation to them. It is important to come with
a willingness to learn. The first thing to be discussed is the
best posture for each one. On this occasion two chose a prayer
stool and three preferred to sit. I think that sitting on an
upright chair is often best, and generally so for the middle-
aged and beyond. Richard Rolle, sometimes called the father
of the mystics of Julian's period, had some lovely words to
say about sitting. 'Sitting,' he would say, 'I am most at rest
and my heart most upward. I have loved to sit for thus I have

loved God more, and I remained longer within the comfort of love than if I were walking or standing or kneeling.'[7]

We have described the rudiments of posture, but there are one or two things to add for the sitting position. The seat should be firm, and the best height is that which allows the thighs to be horizontal when the feet are firmly planted on the ground. If temperature and other circumstances allow it helps to remove one's shoes, thus enabling the feet to relax. A hard chair is best, and a flat seat desirable. Chairs commonly found in churches in which the middle of the seat descends to a point make a good back position more or less impossible. The seat should be sufficiently deep to support the thighs. If the back of the chair slopes backwards we should ignore it. We have said nothing about the arms. They are to be allowed to relax with the hands placed palms downwards on the top of the thighs, or folded gently in the lap. As the tensions in the arms and hands drop away they can be felt to grow warmer. In this position we sit looking to the heart centre for the allotted time.

But someone may ask, what has this to do with prayer? The answer must be that the assuming of our posture becomes prayer from the very moment we *intend* to pray. Too little notice has often been taken of the importance of intention in prayer. When we come to *The Cloud* we shall note that demands are made upon our *attention* in the 'work' the author describes for us. But even prior to that there must be the *intention* to attend, and when attention wanders, as it inevitably must, the prayer goes on so long as the intention remains. When the author tells us we are to mean God and to go on meaning him he is indicating this. But every activity takes its value from its intention. A gift made lovingly may be outwardly indistinguishable from one made grudgingly; it is the intention alone which puts the actions poles apart. If someone says 'O God' without intending to pray, then the words are blasphemy, or impatience, or boredom, or something else. The same words become prayer if the intention to pray is present.

I was referring just now to a group of five young people who came to the Julian Cell for instruction. We began by using the following prayer:

Come *Holy Spirit*, Spirit of Love, Spirit of Discipline,
   In the Silence
Come to us and bring us your peace;
Rest in us that we may be tranquil and still;
Speak to us as each heart needs to hear;
Reveal to us things hidden and things longed for;
Rejoice in us that we may praise and be glad;
Pray in us that we may be at one with you and with each
   other;
Refresh and *Renew* us from your living springs of water;
Dwell in us now and always. Amen.

This prayer was the expression of our intention, and to put our intention or what it should be into words may be a helpful thing to do. Von Hügel once wrote: 'I kiss my child because I love her, and in kissing her I love her more.' I cannot recall whether those words were said in relation to prayer, but there is an exact parallel which may be carried over into vocal prayer. But our point now is that, whether we verbalize our prayer or not, the words are assumed and understood (though not reflected upon) when we come into the silence before God. If we are people who are caught up in the liturgy of the Church, its eucharistic worship and its round of prayer and praise, then inevitably in the stillness we bring all these aspirations with us. They will not be deliberately expressed at this time unless it be in a very simple way—a word or short sentence carried in the heart. Silence takes over where discursive thinking leaves off.

It may be helpful to see the matter like this. By taking up our position for prayer and holding it in the silence—a right intention is assumed—we are doing two things. First we are expressing our desire for God; and secondly (if we may speak in human terms) we are giving God the opportunity in the best manner we know at this particular time of fulfilling that desire. Life is full of parallels. When we lie down at night we express our desire for sleep, and at the same time we are giving sleep its best chance of coming to us. If we are to master any discipline such as learning a language or playing the piano, we express our intention by sitting before our work, and this provides the opportunity for the skill to be given us.

God can, of course, come to us at any time or in any way. The writer can find inspiration on the bus or in the park. Yet normally he has to go through the discipline of sitting down with pen in hand, expecting or at least hoping that as he writes the words will be given him.

'The greatest revelation is stillness.' The words of our chapter heading are taken from the Chinese philosopher Lao-tze. They could be reinforced from many quarters. 'If you become still', wrote Goethe, 'help is always at hand.' So, too, Eckhart: 'God speaks his eternal word only to the truly tranquil soul.' And of Kierkegaard it has been written:

> As his prayer became more and more recollected, he himself had less to say. Finally he became quite still. In his tranquillity he became more than just a non-talker, he became a listener. At first he had believed that to pray meant to talk, but he learnt that prayer was not even silence, it was listening. And so it is: prayer is not hearing oneself talk. Prayer is becoming still, remaining still, and waiting till one hears God.[8]

It was said earlier that *The Cloud* had something extremely interesting to say about posture. It says in effect that if you go to prayer in a bit of a huddle, then as the prayer begins to take hold of you you will find your back straightening out, so that in the end your body will assume the best position for taking its part in the work of the spirit. I find that to be an interesting corroboration of the rightness of the posture we have described. Nature, it is being said, will in any case lead you to it. Body and spirit become partners in one work. The author of *The Cloud* for whom the action of the spirit is primary – the body following where the spirit leads – describes what takes place in the following words:

> For when a soul is determined to engage in this work, then, at the same time (and the contemplative does not notice it) his body, which perhaps before he began tended to stoop because this was easier, now through the Spirit holds itself upright, and follows physically what has been done spiritually. All very fitting![9]

Before we leave the question of posture, we may look at

two additional positions, which I take from St Ignatius in his *Spiritual Exercises*. These are, rather surprisingly, perhaps, from such a source, lying flat on the ground on one's back; or prostrate: lying with face downwards. The second is an outward expression of humility, of our creatureliness before God. You cannot get much lower than that. But it can too greatly revive our energies in bringing an increased blood supply to the head. It is easy, if we have gone to our prayer tired, to fall asleep in this position, but what matter if we do? 'Those who have the gale of the Holy Spirit go forward even in sleep,'[10] says Brother Lawrence. Sleep is an important, though much overlooked way in which the Holy Spirit completes his work in us. Not only is it the great restorer of our physical and mental energies, but it has much to give at the psychological level through nature's mechanism of the dream—independently of whether we can interpret our dreams analytically or not. It cannot be for nothing that God has ordained for most of us that we shall spend more than twenty years of our lives asleep. If we fall asleep when prostrate in prayer, it is best to accept gladly the refreshment sleep brings. Our energies will be greatly renewed for the remainder of the time. St Ignatius' other position—lying on the back—helps, as we have seen, to reduce tensions. Probably nothing more than over-tenseness blocks the free activity of the Holy Spirit. St Ignatius' actual words are these:

> . . . to enter upon the contemplation, at one time kneeling, at another prostrate on the ground, or lying face upwards, or seated, or standing, always intent on seeking that which I desire. Here we will make two observations: first, if kneeling I find that which I desire, I will not change to another position; and if prostrate in like manner, etc.; secondly, in the point in which I find that which I desire, there will I rest without being anxious to proceed farther, until I have satisfied myself.[11]

Having taken up our position we are now to hold it for an appointed time. An hour-glass—so-called, though I am thinking of the models which measure from ten to thirty minutes—can be a handy aid to a flagging will. Even an egg-timer's worth of silence is not to be despised. It is in fact much better to do what is within one's power to attend to realistically than to spend one's time somewhat aimlessly for half an hour. Many will want twenty minutes or rather more, and to mark the time by setting the kitchen clock may be helpful. What needs to be stressed is that a regular ten minutes twice a day, or even five, or less, is better than half an hour snatched occasionally through the month.

It will probably be a recurring temptation to end before the time is up. This is likely to be because it seems that nothing is happening, and that we are simply wasting our time. We are like children who, having planted seeds in their garden plot, think that their work is in vain because they can see no signs of life. But below the surface a great deal is going on, and it is just the same in the silence of prayer. We must understand that just because what is happening is at the level of the unconscious we cannot, by definition, be aware that anything is taking place. And just as a child should measure his gardening attempts by the summer bloom, so the worth of prayer should be assessed, never by how it seems at the time, but by its later fruits. Julian, as we have seen, and *The Cloud*, as we shall see, insist on this, and together with them all the authorities of the spiritual life.

What can be helpful in the presence of this temptation is to see one's prayer as an offering. About an offering there are two important points. One is that it shall be given gladly, willingly and lovingly, and the other is that it doesn't matter whether it succeeds or not in the ordinary sense in which we use that dubious word. An offering has simply to be offered, and we should despise all thoughts such as whether our prayer is strengthening to ourselves or to anybody else. We simply make it as best we can, a free response to the grace given us—for God does not override our freedom—through the Holy Spirit. And we make it—it may help to reflect—not alone but in union with the whole Body of Christ, in both this life and the life beyond.

I remember how as a small boy I bought my father a small earthenware jar. In my eagerness that it should be the first sight on which he should feast his eyes on his birthday morning, I crept into his room in the early hours, and laid it on his bed beside him as he slept. Alas, when I went in later to share his joy, there was my lovely vase—all shilling's worth of it—in a hundred pieces on the floor. I think I must have wept, as my father took me in his arms explaining that it was the love behind the gift which mattered. Then we stooped down and picked up the bits, and he put them on the mantelpiece, saying he would keep them there and value them just as much. I do not know if there are mantelpieces in heaven, but I am sure Julian would have delighted to say that God collects the poor broken fragments of our prayers for love's sake, and treasures them for all that we would have wished them to be.

Yet our offering here is but a part, and it is incomplete unless we see it in the context of prayer within the whole Body of Christ. Hence we return to the importance of our eucharistic background whatever form our prayer may take. The Eucharist is a constant reminder of the corporate nature of our salvation and, moreover, that it is God's action which saves. We do our part, as it were, in coming to church, in responding to the liturgy, in holding out our hands for the bread and wine. It would be pointless to go through the motions if we did not know that, at the end, God has a gift in store. The posture, the stillness, the method, the waiting: these belong to man's endeavour. By these means, aided by grace, we lay ourselves open to the breathing of God's mercy, as the parched earth looks upwards for the rain to fall. The opening of the heavens belongs to him. We can neither command it nor control it. Yet that does not excuse us from doing what we can. St Paul holds these thoughts together in a memorable sentence: 'Work out your own salvation in fear and trembling, for it is God who works in you to will and to do of his own good pleasure.'[12]

The Cloud of Unknowing

We may now turn to *The Cloud of Unknowing* and its important supplement, *The Book of Privy Counsel*. The theme of both books is the way of prayer in the obscurity of faith, without the support of reasoning, memory, imagination or the outward senses. It is a way of darkness and the phrase 'cloud of unknowing' is given to symbolize the experience it describes. In it, the writer urges that 'every speculation of the natural mind is to be utterly and completely rejected and forgotten'.[1]

> See that nothing occupies your thoughts except an utter determination—a naked intent—to reach out to God: no special thought about what he is, or how he works, but only that he is as he is. Let him be himself, please, and nothing else. You are not to go probing into him with your smart and subtle ideas. . . . It is as if you were saying to God, 'What I am, Lord, I offer you. I am not thinking of you in any particular way, except that you are as you are, no more and no less.'[2]

But it is not going to be easy, because

> Your wayward curiosity can find nothing solid to hold on to in a happening of this sort, and so it grumbles and tells you to stop doing it and do something 'useful' . . . (But) on no account go back to the old ways (of discursive meditation), even when they seem good and holy and your mind is inclining thereto.[3]

Both books are written for a young disciple whom we suppose had appealed to the author for teaching on prayer. It is clear, however, that the writer intends his counsel for every reader called the same way. He makes it clear that not all

Christians are so called, though the call may come later in life. In the prologue of *The Cloud* the author stresses the prior need of following the way of Christ as nearly as possible in the active life, with the settled desire to move on to the contemplative way when the call may come. The book is not for the dilettante. There must be a genuine desire to find God; a preparedness for the demands made on one's time and way of life; and a willingness to accept and pass through the suffering it will entail. Christianity, it has been well said, is God's offer to man to have his purgatory in *this* life, and the way of prayer opened up in *The Cloud* is the invitation to enter purgatory—'it is your purgatory'⁴—and by the cleansing and purging action of the Holy Spirit to be taken to the blessedness of life which lies beyond. Tradition has it that Jesus said, 'He that is near me is near the fire.'

The author's way may perhaps be best described by an extensive quotation from his writing. To make for easier reading, the chapter sources are not given in the passage which follows, and further, it is arranged as a piece of continuous prose. It should be noted that the sentences are not necessarily consecutive in the original, nor do they always appear in the same order in *The Cloud* itself. The liberty has been taken of moving forwards or backwards from one chapter to another in order to summarize the teaching more clearly.

Lift up your heart to God with humble love; and mean God and not what you get out of him. Hate to think of anything but God himself, so that nothing occupies your mind or will but only God. Try to forget all created things. Let them go, and pay no attention to them. Do not give up but work away. When you begin you find only darkness and a cloud of unknowing. Reconcile yourself to wait in this darkness as long as is necessary, but go on longing after him you love. Strike that thick cloud of unknowing with the sharp dart of longing love, and on no account think of giving up. You are to reach out with a naked intention directed towards God and him alone. Mean God who created you, and bought you, and graciously called you to this state of life. Let some such word as 'God' or 'love', or some other word given to you, be fixed to your heart so that it is always there come what may. It will be your shield and spear in peace and war alike. If God leads you to certain words my advice is not to let them go, that is, if you are using words at all in your prayer. Should any thought arise and obtrude itself in the darkness, asking what you are seeking, and what you are wanting, answer that it is God you want: 'Him I covet, him I seek, and him alone.'

Just as this cloud of unknowing is, as it were, above you and between you and God, so you must put a cloud of forgetting between you and all creation. Everything must be hidden under this cloud of forgetting. Indeed, if we may say so reverently, when we are engaged in this work it profits little or nothing to think even of God's kindness or worth, or of our Lady, or of the saints and angels, or of the joys of heaven. It may be good sometimes to think particularly about God's kindness and worth, yet in the work before us it must be put down and covered with the cloud of forgetting.

When you have done all you can to make the proper amendment laid down by Holy Church, then get to work quick sharp! If memories of your past actions keep coming between you and God, or any new thought or sinful impulse, you are resolutely to step over them because of your deep love for God. Try to cover them with the thick cloud of forgetting. And if it is really hard work you can use every dodge, scheme and spiritual stratagem you can find to put them away. Do everything you can to act as if you did not know that these thoughts were strongly pushing in between you and God. Try to look over their shoulders, seeking something else—which is God, shrouded in the cloud of unknowing.[5]

In stark brevity we have here the heart of *The Cloud*. The quotation taken alone makes an excellent starting-point, though naturally it is no substitute for reading the book itself. The passage illustrates, incidentally, not only the author's teaching but his vivid and lively style, and his capacity for expressing himself clearly and concisely. For this reason commentary can be brief, at least until we reach the second half of the passage dealing with the cloud of forgetting, which will call for discussion and development.

In the silence, then, we are to reach out to God in faith with the naked intent of the will, lovingly and generously, and we are to mean God and to go on meaning him, using, if it will help, a word such as 'God' or 'love' or a short sentence to act as a focal point. And it is stressed that we shall persevere. The passage suggests there will be rough and difficult times when we are tempted to give up. But we are to go on, resolute in will, paying no attention to our feelings which if they had their way would take us to some easier task. What of the darkness we shall encounter? We are to reconcile ourselves to wait in it as long as is necessary, and to reach out in will and intent towards God shrouded, as the writer puts it, in the cloud of unknowing.

The author, however, introduces a second cloud, and this he calls the cloud of forgetting. We are to put a cloud of forgetting between ourselves and all creation, and everything is to be hidden under it. We are to try to forget all created things, and with this cloud to cover all intruding thoughts. The language is clear and uncompromising, and yet it is mild compared with other things the writer has to say. Thus he tells us—it is not in our quotation—that if a thought intrudes itself we are to say to it, 'Get down', and to trample on it for the love of God.[6] Further we are told to 'suppress these insidious thoughts',[7] and warned that a thought may be a sin if not quickly put down.[8] Most strongly of all we are to trample past memories under foot, and as often as they come up to push them down.[9]

It may well be that we are alarmed by the vigour of the writer's language. We shall at once want to ask whether it is possible to do what is urged upon us. From our experience we shall almost certainly say that it is not possible to prevent thoughts, fantasies and memories from entering consciousness during prayer; and further, that once they have entered the imagination they cannot by an act of will be dispelled. If an aeroplane flies overhead you cannot but hear it, you cannot keep yourself from being conscious of the smell of food as it floats in from the kitchen, and a touch on the shoulder cannot pass unnoticed. How should it be otherwise with thoughts which drift in through the imagination without the stimulus of the senses? We are, however, in posing these questions pressing the writer further than he would go. A fuller reading of *The Cloud* will satisfy us that the most he wants us to do is to exercise control so far as we can over the stream of consciousness which bids to sweep across the mind in the time of prayer.

If we turn to chapter 10 from which we shall now quote freely, we shall see that there are two types of thought the writer has in mind. There is first of all 'the spontaneous thought, springing to mind unsought and unwittingly'.[10] This, he says, will be a part of everybody's experience every time he goes to prayer. It is, moreover, a type of thought which 'cannot be reckoned to be sin' though the observation follows that it may be due to original sin, meaning, as we shall agree, that our fallen state has a great deal to do in determining the thoughts—in both variety and intensity—which are likely to come unbidden to the mind in the time of prayer. The writer is speaking here of what is generally termed involuntary distraction, that is to say the type of distraction in which the will plays no part. Our prayer goes wrong, says *The Cloud*, when we give our attention to such thoughts, thus (in the terms we are using) turning an involuntary distraction into one which is voluntary. Voluntary distraction, then, belongs to the second type of thinking.

The writer then goes on to speak of what he has in mind. It may, for example, be pleasant thoughts which seek to grasp our attention, and these are dealt with at the end of the chapter under the headings of pride, avarice, gluttony and lust. Thus it may be—to take our own example—that we have been praised for some piece of work we have done, and in our prayer time the remembrance comes to mind, and we dwell on it, and take pleasure in it, and enlarge upon it with some measure of self-congratulation. Such indulgence—in contrast to offering what we have been enabled to do in a simple moment of thanksgiving, and turning again to our way of prayer—would come under the heading of pride. 'If this thought that you deliberately conjure up, or harbour (once it has spontaneously risen) and dwell lovingly upon, is natural worth or knowledge, charm or station, favour or beauty,—

then it is *Pride*.' We can extend for ourselves the author's thinking into the other three categories which he gives. In every case it is true that the spontaneous arising of the thought is not sin, but to 'dwell on it, and in the end to fix your heart and will on it, and turn to it for nourishment'—this is to be reckoned as sin. 'You think at such times that you want never better than to live in peace and quiet with this pleasant thing.'

It is not only the pleasant things which may seek to take possession of us. It may be that some grudge we have harboured comes up at the time of prayer, a 'grouse over something that grieves you, or has grieved you'. To be aware of this involuntary distraction is one thing, but to give one's willing attention to it and to enlarge upon it is another, for

if you allow houseroom to this thing that you naturally like or grouse about ... ultimately it will take root in your inmost being, in your will, and with the consent of your will. Then it is deadly sin. This happens whenever you, or any of those I have been speaking of, deliberately conjure up (voluntary distraction as we would say) the memory of somebody or something or other.

The writer deals briefly with what he has now in mind under the headings of anger, envy and sloth. Once again we are to stress that it is not the spontaneous arising of thoughts, but the voluntary dwelling upon them which is to be resisted. Hence we may explain the vigour of *The Cloud*'s language which occupied our thinking earlier on.

Let us now turn to these spontaneous thoughts which may present themselves during the time of prayer. What are we to do with them? If, for example, I have a fear lurking below consciousness, and if in the silence it steals into the mind—as it well may—am I to try to suppress it? Let it be agreed (with *The Cloud*) that we are not to encourage its entry, and that if it does enter we are not to examine it, or develop it, or follow it. But are we to try to push it out, and if we do will it do any good? Will this not merely serve to fasten our minds on it, or if we succeed for a brief period, will it not come back a little later with renewed force? Would it not be better to let it float in the periphery of the mind or, if it must, to rest on the mind as a sort of dull weight, rather like a headache, recognized but unexamined and unattended to, we meanwhile occupying ourselves with the word or sentence or whatever may be the focal point of our prayer? In going to prayer we have put ourselves into God's hands, and may it not be that this fear at the touch of the Holy Spirit is now presenting itself for the work of healing to be done upon it? May not detachment and release be a better attitude than suppression?

Or if, to come nearer to *The Cloud*'s example, I have a buried resentment which presents itself in the silence, am I to try to push it back to the place whence it came? May not this be what Jung would have called a part of my shadow self, a revelation of the darker side of my nature which I do not like, and take pains to conceal from others and prefer to hide even from myself? If it is kept down, unrecognized and unfaced, will it not too be unhealed? Is not this the chance for the healing process to be taken forward, for the unconscious to yield up a part of what lies in its depths to be integrated with the conscious mind to the enrichment and enlargement of the whole?

I believe that what is here suggested is true, and that although it may appear to be in conflict with some of the language of *The Cloud* which we have quoted earlier, further examination will show that that is not so. For although the author says, and says with vigour, that thoughts and memories are to be put away, he distinguishes, as we have seen, sharply between the spontaneous unbidden thoughts which will be the experience of 'every recollection', and the voluntary ones over which we have a measure of control. Our suggestion that the type of distraction we have outlined is for our healing is, in fact, fully in accord with the teaching of *The Cloud*. Moreover, we are all in this together, not just the young man of twenty-four for whom he is writing but all of us, for 'though now I am teaching you, in all truth I know that I still have a very long way to go myself'. And the writer at once goes on to say, echoing what we have written above, that we are here at a point of healing. For, as we remarked earlier, he likens the experience to purgatory, of which the mark is cleansing through the right acceptance and endurance of suffering:

Endure with all humility any suffering you have to endure. . . . In truth it is your purgatory; when the pain has
passed, and the skills have been given by God, and, by his
grace, have become habitual, then without doubt you will
have been cleansed not only from sin, but also from the
suffering it causes.[11]

Thus, in the author's view contemplative prayer works the
most fundamental work of all in the soul. In chapter 28 he
expresses this directly by saying that in contemplation 'the
root and ground' of sin is dried up. It is not (to use our own
example) a matter of chopping off the heads of the weeds as
they push themselves up between the paving stones, but of
attacking them at their roots with the aim of eradicating them
altogether. This is the process which is always being taken
forward in the 'work' which the author sets before us.

Before we pass on it will be well to note the *Cloud*-author's
conviction that the healing work of which we have spoken is
effective not for ourselves alone, but is something in which all
men are in some degree caught up. We are not self-contained
units and we cannot separate ourselves as though we were
islands set here and there in a universal sea. We need an
organic picture, such as St Paul gives us of the body, in which
the healthy functioning of each part has its effect for good on
the body as a whole. And so it is that the author of *The Cloud*
can write:

All saints and angels rejoice over it, and hasten to help it
on with all their might. . . . Moreover, the whole of man-
kind is wonderfully helped by what you are doing, in ways
you do not understand. Yes, the very souls in purgatory
find their pain eased by virtue of your work. And in no
better way can you yourself be made clean or virtuous than
by attending to this.[12]

Thus we are to be encouraged to persevere. We can never
know, at least in this life, the extent to which we may help
one another by faithfulness in the way God has called us.

*

The way is now clear for us to examine what to do with
memories as they steal into consciousness during prayer. The

Cloud-author is content to give us two 'dodges', adding that there are others which we may discover for ourselves. The first is quite a simple one:

> Do everything you can to act as if you did not know (the thoughts) were so strongly pushing in between you and God. Try to look, as it were, over their shoulders, seeking something else—which is God, shrouded in the cloud of un-knowing. If you do so, I believe that you will soon find your hard work much easier. I believe that if this dodge is looked at in the right way, it will be found to be nothing else than a longing and desire for God, to feel and see of him what one may here below.[13]

This simple illutration opens up one experience in prayer. I imagine myself to be at a football match, anxious to watch the game, but the man in front is just too tall. I manage to look over his shoulder and all my attention is on the game. Yet I cannot help being aware of him, and I do not try to pretend that he is not there. It is no good escaping from the realities of the situation. So too, in prayer, I look beyond the distraction, but I am not afraid to recognize it, and I accept it for as long as it remains.

The second dodge which the author gives is at first sight a surprising one, and if we have not experienced its power we may be inclined to question its wisdom. We shall, however, miss something of great importance if we do not heed it. Once again we may let *The Cloud* speak in its lively and picturesque way:

> There is another spiritual dodge to try if you wish. When you feel that you are completely powerless to put these thoughts away, cower down before them like some cringing captive overcome in battle, and reckon that it is ridiculous to fight against them any longer. In this way you surrender yourself to God while you are in the hands of your enemies, and feeling that you have been overcome for ever. Please pay special heed to this suggestion, for I think that if you try it out it will dissolve every opposition. I am quite sure that if this dodge, too, can be looked at in the right way, it will be recognised to be none other than the true

knowledge and experience of the self you are; wretched, filthy, and far worse than nothing. Such knowledge and experience is humility. And this humility causes God himself to come down in his might, and avenge you of your enemies, and take you up, and fondly dry your spiritual eyes—just as a father would act towards his child, who had been about to die in the jaws of wild boar, or mad, devouring bears![14]

This discerning and revealing passage may be rightly linked with what has been said earlier of the cleansing and healing possibilities which were opened up, as buried thoughts and emotions rise to consciousness during prayer. The writer is clearly implying that the experience is necessary if we are to grow in self-knowledge and be progressively grounded in humility. The 'unpeace' in ourselves has to surface if it is to be rightly dealt with. We note, however, that the author says that in our utter helplessness we do not surrender to our enemies, but to God in the hands of our enemies. It is possible in such situations to surrender to self-pity or depression or fear, to mention only three of the various emotions which may clamour for attention. That way, as we know, lies despair and ultimately destruction. Clouds and darkness are indeed round about us, and in the midst of it all we are to surrender unconditionally into the arms of God. If only—and the suggestion is there—we could at such times penetrate the reality of such situations with the eye of faith, they would become occasions for hope rather than despair. Just when we think we are moving to a breakdown, God may be taking us to a breakthrough.

This trustful surrender of which *The Cloud* speaks is nowhere better illustrated than in the writings of Jean-Pierre de Caussade, widely known today for his treatise *Self Abandonment to Divine Providence*. His letters to the Sisters of the Visitation— for whom he was confessor and director—are unfortunately much less known, and, sadly, they have been out of print in English for a long while. It would be fascinating if we had the Sisters' side of the correspondence, but their letters have not survived. We are left to imagine how one after another would write to describe the interior trials through which she

was passing—temptations, doubts, fears, scruples, humiliations, spiritual darkness—all that the Holy Spirit has to
take us through before the death to self is completed. Often
the Sisters must have asked for his prayers. We may be sure
that they had them, but not always on the lines they had
hoped, for it was his way to write that nothing would induce
him to pray for relief for, although he knew well what trials
they were passing through, he could see clearly what to them
was hidden, the greatness of the work God was doing and the
depth of the operation of the Holy Spirit at such times. An
extract from one letter must stand for many passages which
might have been chosen:

> When I think of the infinite value of your present tribula-
> tions I dare not wish for them to end ... I already see
> plainly the rich harvest reaped in your soul by the ordeal
> through which God has made you pass. Although it has
> brought down violent storms upon you interiorly I cannot
> doubt that it has helped your spiritual progress very
> greatly. Through it you have learnt to be crucified in-
> teriorly, to find all things repugnant, to make God constant
> and painful sacrifices, to discipline yourself in many things,
> to acquire patience, to become submissive, and to abandon
> yourself to God.[15]

The letter continues for several pages. Here, in what this
Sister is passing through and in the way she is directed to
respond, we have clothed in the words of a great spiritual
director what *The Cloud* is saying in the second of its images,
the surrender to God in the hands of one's enemies.

This second image may also be a valuable ally in times of
sickness. We have spoken of the importance of posture, and
of how the body may assist the spirit on its way, but all the
time we have assumed that the one who prays is physically
fit and strong. In times of sickness and suffering we do not
pray less well because we cannot assume an upright posture,
nor yet because we cannot follow the directions of *The Cloud*
which we have given earlier. It will not now be a case of
reaching out with a naked intent towards God, seeking him
in the thick cloud of unknowing—which even a mild temperature or headache make impossible—but of surrendering

ourselves into God's hands in the presence of these our enemies. The very offering of infirmity or suffering betokened by the act of surrender is itself the prayer. This was the prayer of Julian as in pain and weakness she trusted herself to God in the period which led to her showings. It was, too, the prayer of Jesus on the cross and its redemptive power extends beyond anything we can imagine.[16]

12

Distractions are for Healing

In the last chapter we spoke of two 'dodges' given by the author of *The Cloud* by which we may deal with distracting thoughts in the time of prayer. The first was to try to look over the shoulder of these thoughts to God, who lay beyond. The second was to surrender oneself to God in their presence; and we may add that it will help to make it as far as possible a matter of indifference whether they go or not. The first belongs chiefly to the beginning and early stages of prayer; the second will be increasingly called for as prayer becomes more passive.

The object of the two dodges, and of others which *The Cloud* says we may discover for ourselves, is to assist the ever restless mind to settle down, so that in the nakedness of faith, unhampered by the dissipating effects of conceptual thinking, all its energies may be gathered into the seeking of God in the cloud of unknowing. Yet, for the mind to settle, it is no good trying to drive away one's thoughts, but rather must they be allowed to die down of their own accord. We may be helped if we have in our minds the picture of a rotating fly-wheel. The wheel, we shall suppose, is energized by our thinking, so that to think discursively during prayer—and this includes the examining and developing of involuntary distractions—is to add to the rotation speed of the wheel. As our object is to allow the wheel to come to rest, our temptation, when we discover ourselves pursuing a line of thought, is to try not to think. This, we may imagine, will surely have the opposite effect; it will put a brake on the wheel and help its rotation to cease. A little reflection, however, will show that this will not be so. For to try not to think is once again a form of thinking, our thought this time being directed to the concept of 'not-thinking'. Thus we reach the position of seeing that to put energy into thinking is a hindrance to the slowing down of the wheel, and to put it into not-thinking is no better. Neither will help to bring the wheel to rest; on the contrary each will help it to go faster. Hence we arrive at two sentences we may say quietly to ourselves from time to time during prayer. The first is 'Do not try to think'; the second is 'Do not try not to think'. The process has to be worked out in practice, and only the principles can be grasped from the written page. It must be stressed, and we have discussed why it should be so, that 'Do not try to think' is quite different from 'Try not to think', which will increase the speed of the wheel; and 'Do not try not to think' is again quite different from 'Try to think', which again only increases its speed.

What we have described is known as *shikantaza*, a form of meditation to which I was introduced at a Zen Buddhist retreat conducted by two Zen monks. The sentence perhaps needs qualifying, for most of us were Christians, with a large proportion of Roman Catholic laity, priests and religious, and Mass was a feature of every day. The working day was, however, given over entirely to Zen meditation and practice; and *shikantaza*, which means literally 'just sitting', was the form of meditation we were taught. It may be helpful to go inside the meditation room and listen to the Roshi as he spoke to us. After instructing us on posture, the principles of which we have already described in an earlier chapter, the Roshi set us around the room looking towards the wall, and about five feet from it. With eyes open we were simply to 'sit', a technical term to cover whatever form of posture was chosen. Some preferred the lotus posture with the help of the Zen cushion, others to sit on a prayer stool placed as a bridge across the calves,[1] and one or two an upright chair. When we had taken up our positions, a light beat on a gong marked the beginning of the meditation. The Roshi would watch us, correct us if the posture lapsed or if we fidgeted or turned the head, and would encourage us with words from time to time. Chiefly came the sentences, 'Do not try to think' and 'Do not try not to think'. This pattern, however, was extended on occasions to cover the whole sensory experience. Thus as an aeroplane flew overhead: 'Do not try to hear it' and 'Do not try not to hear it'. The wall was papered—ideally it should be blank—and one person had said shapes kept forming and holding her attention. Then: 'Do not try to see' and 'Do not try not to see'. Was it the scent of flowers coming through the window? 'Do not try to smell' and 'Do not try not to smell'. Or how about that ache in the knee or shoulders? 'Do not try to feel it' and 'Do not try not to feel it'. After half an hour we were told to rise for *kinhin,* a way of meditative walking which it is not our purpose to describe here.

But inevitably thoughts, memories and imaginations would arise. What had the Roshi to say of these? 'Do not be afraid of them. Do not develop them, and do not follow them. Let them ascend to the Lord of the Temple. They are there for your healing.' I have already indicated in our discussion of *The Cloud* that I believe we need to pay special attention to those last words. The whole quotation is important, but with most of it we are familiar. Of involuntary distractions, however, it is too often said that if they are not attended to they will pass without doing any harm. But this view is too negative. These memories and imaginations presenting themselves from the unconscious at the touch of the Holy Spirit are there for our healing. This encouraging and positive view is, as we have seen, taken by *The Cloud,* and it was interesting for me to find in Zen its confirmation. It is true that not all distractions have the source we have just indicated. Involuntary distraction may be caused by a passing car or a neighbour's radio or physical discomfort, to mention only a few of the commoner sort. Or it may arise from fields of psychic force set up by others near or far, and some will be much more sensitive in this way than others. Or yet again there may be interference from demonic sources for, as St Paul reminds us, we do not fight against flesh and blood, but against principalities and powers and spiritual wickedness in high places.[2] But the commonest distraction at this time is likely to be through the opening up of the unconscious, allowing memories and imaginations to seep through into the mind. Normally these are held back from consciousness to a greater or lesser extent by the ordinary processes of thinking, and talking, and working. In prayer they are released rather as memories and emotions are released in dreams as we sleep, though the illustration must not be pressed too far for in sleep we lose all conscious measure of control. We have here in our prayer a loosening or releasing of repressions, and it may be that some of them are deeply emotionally charged. Fears, greeds, doubts, envies, resentments, passions may all at one time or another find their way in in the silence. We are not to encourage this intrusion, but neither are we to run away from it. In Jungian terms we are being brought into contact with our shadow selves, the darker side of our nature which we ignore at our peril, but brought in contact not that we may be diminished, but that what is good may be integrated into consciousness, that we may enter into a deeper freedom, wholeness and completeness in Christ.

In what has been described we have a process which is going on in all life which seeks to be open to the Holy Spirit. But very especially is this process of integration at work in the time of prayer. This encounter with the unconscious is an important part of every person's growth to maturity. As we have seen in an earlier chapter, Jung sees the unconscious as a source of power, and that if we keep forces in it altogether repressed two things are going to happen. The first is that we shall deny ourselves much of the power which might be ours. This is because mental energy is engaged in holding the repression down, making less energy available for the ordinary needs of life. The second is that we shall invite the hostility of these forces, which may now become dangerous and break out, generally unrecognized for what they are, in inconvenient and perhaps distressing and anti-social ways.

In his book *The Still Point,* William Johnston, a Jesuit priest who has learnt much from the practice of Zen, describes (drawing on Jung) what is happening as thoughts rise to consciousness during Zen meditation.

As a therapist Jung was chiefly attracted by the healing powers of Zen. He often speaks of psychic wholeness accruing from its practice. As conflict was caused by disharmony between the conscious and unconscious mind, so this was solved by the rising up of unconscious elements. For this eruption was not an indiscriminate something popping up from the mysterious depths, but is rather (Jung's words) 'the unexpected, comprehensive, completely illuminating answer to the problems of one's psychic life.' Hence the resulting equilibrium and peace. Zen helps the development of healthy psychic growth, since in its silent darkness the unconscious is allowed to rise up, thus creating a deep and wealthy conscious life.[3]

Yet not everyone is ready to deal with the forces which may emerge during silent prayer. If the ego structure is weak, they may be as an erupting volcano swamping the conscious mind and making it impossible for the person to contain them. Hence we may see the wisdom of the Christian tradition in insisting that the call to contemplative prayer is a distinct call within the Christian life. The building up of a firm and stable ego is the first need, belonging to the earlier stage of life; only then can the contemplative call be received without the risk of disintegration. For those who can receive it, on the other hand, it is the way of integration, or individuation, to use the term associated with Jung. This word has been defined, as we have seen, as 'the conscious realisation and integration of all the possibilities immanent in the individual'.

Jung is saying in his own idiom in relation to Zen what the author of *The Cloud*, and de Caussade in his letters, are saying in their terms in relation to Christian prayer. What arises from the depths whether in Christian prayer or in Zen, what in Christian terms we call involuntary distraction, is to be seen as a friend offering something to the conscious life for integration with it, and consequently for its enrichment and enlargement. Hence we are never to receive involuntary distractions, which by definition do not have the encouragement of the will, with feelings of guilt, for under God they are presented for our healing. I have written elsewhere:

It may help to see the Holy Spirit as an all wise psychotherapist who takes his patient now to one point, now to another in the movement towards integration and wholeness. Sometimes we can see clearly why this or that is chosen, but at other times we must be content to wait in the darkness, and trust his better wisdom. There is no need for us to know. . . . All that is necessary is that we are assured that this is a healing point, for we can then approach involuntary distractions in a positive way, instead of seeing them as spoiling our prayer, or worse still receiving them with feelings of guilt as though we had an indication that we have not properly fulfilled our part.[4]

We may now turn to ask how we are to deal with the memories and imaginations—what we classify generally as involuntary distractions—which may present themselves to the conscious mind during the time of prayer. We must remember here that we are not simply speaking of thoughts and memories which may be difficult or painful, but of all thoughts and imaginations. Recollection of things beautiful and 'serene, memories of happy friendships, scriptural and devotional thoughts—what *The Cloud* calls 'thoughts of God's kindness and worth'—are all to be treated in the same way at this time, that is to say, in the imagery of *The Cloud*, they are to be put under the cloud of forgetting. This is a difficult saying for some, but it is important that we should be clear before we proceed. If we liken our prayer to the flight of a bird we may say that we are as effectively restrained by a silken cord as by a rough string. It will be proper to reflect at other times—and *The Cloud* acknowledges this—on all that we have mentioned. It is simply that we are not to do so now.

Let us now be practical, and set down some rules for our guidance when a thought arises spontaneously during prayer. It is best to be specific and take some particular distraction, and we can make our own general application later on. We shall suppose, then, that, all unbidden, a fear steals into consciousness. It may be something specific, let us say a fear of heights or of travelling by air, or of open or closed spaces, or of mixing with crowds of people, or it may be just a 'boden misshapen sullen dread', of what we cannot say. What now should our rules be?

(1) Accept the situation with hope. It is not for destruction but for healing.
(2) We have not encouraged the fear to come, and we do not encourage it now that it is here.
(3) We do not try not to think of it. To do so will only fasten our attention on it the more. (Try for ten seconds *not* to think of a five-pound note!)

(4) We do not run away from the fear as though we feared it. That is like running from a bully who will but chase us the more.

(5) We do not deceive ourselves and pretend it is not there. But if we are able to see the situation as 'fear is rising in me', rather than as 'I am afraid', that will help towards detachment from it.

(6) We continue to look to God strongly and firmly, returning to our word, our sentence, our icon (of which more in the next chapter), or whatever may be the focal point of our prayer. If we are using the first image of *The Cloud* we go on looking over the shoulder of the thought; if the second image we continue surrendered to God in its presence; if we are using the Zen way described earlier we go on 'just sitting', looking towards the wall and following the way described. Straining will not help, but we are not to be afraid of hard work. 'Keep on then, and work at it as hard and as fast as you can, I beg you.'[5]

(7) We recognize the fear but we do nothing to analyse it, or develop it, or pursue it. It is handed over to God, and we allow it to go when it will, how it will, if it will. We are to be content to allow the fear to 'float' on the periphery of consciousness or, if it will, to float out of consciousness altogether. 'Floating' is an important word in schools of therapy. 'Let your anxieties float', we are told. We may see the fear as a sort of detached observer of it; what is important is that we do not follow it or develop it. If the situation we are in is painful—and in some measure it will be so—we are to be content to bear that pain as we might any physical discomfort. 'This is your purgatory' says *The Cloud*, that is to say, though painful it has within it the potential for growth, development and healing. (However, if the fear is crippling and persistent, we may need to come to grips with it in another way outside the time of prayer, perhaps with the help of a friend or a skilled counsellor.)

The rules have been set out with a particular type of distraction in mind, one moreover which few people have not known from time to time. They may easily be adapted to cover every situation. But we should remember that if what distracts us is naturally pleasing and attractive, the temptation now is not to run from it but to go along with it. As we have seen in the previous chapter, *The Cloud* deals with these at the end of its chapter 10. We need to remind ourselves that the promise of life in following up the distraction is a deceit. The rules given, whether the distraction is painful or pleasant, make for a spirit of detachment, which in turn makes for the growth of our liberty in Christ to which we are called. What is naturally pleasing is best offered in a spirit of thanksgiving.

I have collected over the years a number of pictures illustrating what others have said on the subject of involuntary distraction during prayer. One may help at one time, another later on. It may be useful to bring them together here. They will present us with a variety of images, each with its own point of appeal.

A desert father says that in the moment that one replies to a distraction it becomes more formidable, and advises his disciple not to be troubled by the thought, nor to try to reply to it, nor to leave it the least possibility of entry. 'But', he adds, 'if it does enter, let it ascend to the Father and say, "As for you I have nothing to do with you. Here is my father, he knows." ' The member of the contemplative order who sent me this illustration added, 'Not then suppression, nor examination, nor encouragement, but release.'

Evagrius of Pontus (fourth century) says that prayer is a laying aside of thoughts, and on this Kallistos Ware comments: 'A laying aside, not a savage conflict, not a furious repression, but a gentle yet persistent act of detachment. Through the repetition of the Name we are helped to lay aside, to let go our trivial or pernicious imaginations, and to replace them with the thought of Jesus.'[6]

St Teresa says that 'it is not good for us to be disturbed by our thoughts or to worry about them in the slightest', and adds a little later: 'The clacking old mill must keep on going round and we must grind our own flour.'[7]

Michael McLean writes: 'Most of our time will be spent sweeping the leaves from the path down which the Lord may come.'[8]

Maria Boulding, OSB, writes:

(Distractions) seem to promise life, while prayer is boring
and empty and a losing of our ego-life. If we grab at them
and follow them we are refusing to be poor and seeking to
'save our life', but helplessness in the grip of involuntary
distractions while the will stands firm is a real poverty of
spirit.[9]

A favourite illustration comes from Zen. You are to imagine
yourself on a bridge spanning a river. You stand there looking
over the parapet straight down into the water as it flows
beneath the bridge. This represents the ordinary stream of
consciousness as it passes across the mind. Coming down the
river are empty boats, and these stand for our distractions.
The boats float down with the stream and pass under the
bridge. Zen says, 'You are to watch the boats, but you are to
resist the temptation to jump on board.'

A friend once gave me this picture, which may be helpful.
Distractions, she said, are like a goldfish in a bowl rising to
the surface. For a few seconds it remains and then vanishes.
So for a brief period we see our distractions out of a corner
of the mind, and they vanish as mysteriously as they came.

Fénelon says we are ever to be plunging ourselves anew
into the ocean of God's love and calls this forgetting of self
the most perfect penitence 'because all conversion consists
only in renouncing self to be engrossed in God'.

De Caussade several times in his letters gives a picture well
worth developing. Enlarging upon his illustration, you see
yourself as waist-deep in the sea with stones in your hands,
and you open your hands and let the stones fall into the sea
and disappear beneath the waters. It is a simple matter of
letting go. I need to extend this, and to say that these stones
may sometimes behave like rubber balls and float round me
when released. The point to note now is that I keep my hands
open. I do not grab again what has been let go. I simply
leave them to be taken away by the tide or not, as the case
may be. There is a valuable literal application here. The very
action of keeping the hands open (literally so) helps to release
thoughts and tensions. What we have described is, however,
only one side. We are, too, to work away on making contrary

reflections, turning to God to make new acts of trust and abandonment.

A Chinese proverb has it that you cannot prevent birds from flying round your head, but that you can prevent them from making nests in your hair.

No illustration can give the whole situation. But each as we consider it can yield something useful. And for many it can be a great help to work with pictures rather than continuous prose.

We have spoken entirely of distractions which arise through the opening up of the unconscious. What are we to say of others? For a certain type of distraction, such as the sudden memory of a letter which has to be written, or of something which has to be bought, it may be a help to have a pencil and paper at hand. The matter can then be jotted down and forgotten. Moving to a deeper level we may ask what we are to do with distractions if they come from a demonic source, such as we remarked earlier? First we may ask whether it is possible to tell the source from which the distraction comes. The answer must be that generally it is not possible, but that that does not matter. What is important is to know how to deal with it, and that will be the same as in the cases we have considered in which thoughts present themselves through the loosening of repressions in the unconscious. We are to continue in our way of prayer, whether in the first or second image of *The Cloud,* or in some other way, and in every case the distraction is to be seen as handed over, given to God to be taken care of. Meanwhile in the power of grace we are content to suffer the disturbance until it is relieved.[10]

What are we to do if the distraction in prayer is one of noise? It may not always be practicable to move to another place, but even if it is we need not be too particular. For all distractions act in another way to that described. In the same way as any other challenge in life, without which we would grow weak and flabby, they serve as strengtheners of the will which overcomes them. This is obviously not to say we should seek out noisy places, but simply that if one has the resolution to persevere in difficult situations the experience will be rewarding.

There is, however, a completely different way of dealing

with noise, a method often used in Zen. It works on the principle that the best way to be rid of your enemy is to make him into your friend. Thus if a ticking clock is disturbing in the time of prayer, instead of taking it to another room you are resolved to listen to every tick so that not a single one escapes you. It thus becomes your point of focus as a word or sentence might be in other circumstances. It makes a very good practice to become still for a few minutes, resolved to listen to every sound around you: the birds singing, the cars passing, a tin dropped in the street, someone sawing wood, a movement in the flat above—these are the noises I heard during a pause before writing the last sentence. A similar plan can be followed with the other senses. In Zen you may be told to put all your awareness into the pain between your shoulders or elsewhere, saying quietly to yourself from time to time, 'paining, paining, paining. . .', in which way the discomfort will become less troublesome and in time may disappear altogether.

It is, however, about distractions arising spontaneously in the silence from below the threshold of consciousness that this chapter is mainly concerned. Met in the power of the Holy Spirit these have a special place in the healing of our disfigured human nature. There is a Jewish saying which runs, 'By your very wounds I will heal you.' Julian herself must have been thinking in some such way as this, when in chapter 39 of her *Revelations* she wrote that our 'wounds' shall be our 'worships'. 'The reward', she tells us, will be 'great, glorious, and honourable'; and 'so shall all our shame be turned into honour and joy'.

The Help of the Senses

I set my eyes on the same cross in which I had seen comfort before, my tongue to speaking of Christ's Passion and repeating the faith of Holy Church, and my heart to clinging to God with all my trust and strength.[1]

The passage refers to Julian's experience in a time of special trial at the end of her sixteenth and last revelation. Her prayer continued thus, she tells us, through the night and until a little after sunrise. There had been an interval of a number of hours between her final showing and the fifteen which preceded it, and the words 'in which I had seen comfort before' most naturally refer back to the beginning of her showings when her parish priest, expecting her to die at any moment, was holding the crucifix before her face. She tells us that she fixed her eyes upon it, after which her sight began to fail, 'and the room became dark about me, as if it were night, except for the image of the cross which somehow was lighted; up but how was beyond my comprehension'.[2] The cross had later been placed at the foot of her bed,[3] and this is where it would now have been as she looked upon it after her final revelation.

Whether Julian was in the habit of praying in this way we cannot say, but it is not unreasonable to suppose that what was a life-line to her on this occasion was a regular feature of her prayers. There must be a strong measure of probability that simply to gaze upon the crucifix, with or without vocal prayer, was throughout a part of the pattern of her devotional life. Certainly we can be helped if we make it or something like it a pattern of our own.

Not everyone will choose a crucifix, though most of us will

see it as having a special claim at least at one season of the Church's year. A group to which I once belonged would use among other forms a bowl of water signifying baptism, a loaf of bread as a eucharistic symbol, or a lighted candle representing Christ as the light of the world. Many who have access to church or chapel gaze, as did the peasant of Ars, upon the tabernacle on the altar—'I look at Him and He looks at me'—and ask for nothing more. Others may be familiar with the use of icons and I myself have in my room four icons representing the fundamentals of the faith: incarnation, cross and passion, resurrection, and Holy Trinity. We associate icons perhaps particularly with the Orthodox Church, for whom they are an integral part of the pattern of the liturgy, supplementing and reinforcing in visual form what is otherwise given in prayer and the reading of the Scriptures. 'That which the word communicates by sound the painting shows silently by representation.'[4] In the Western Church we largely miss what this dimension brings to the richness of worship, taking us beyond words into the silence of the heart before God. Icons are seen by the Orthodox Church as powerful means of the divine grace and as means through which the saints exercise their beneficent powers, whether in healing or exorcism or other blessings of various kinds.

The word icon is simply the Greek for picture, though today it has come to mean a special kind of picture interpreted within the tradition of the Church.[5] Artistically it is also special, for it is designed in what is known as 'reverse perspective', which means that the picture does not disappear into the background, as does, for example, the Constable reproduction before me as I write, but instead the figures are represented so as to project themselves outwards towards the viewer. Another special feature is that there are no shadows in icons. This is because they are conceived as possessing their own interior light which shines out to shed its radiance on those around.

Before we come to talk of praying before icons we may note two practical points. The first is that they can normally be bought—we are speaking of reproductions—in matt or glossy finish. A glossy surface may cause problems for reflection, and a matt surface is preferable for prayer. Secondly, in positioning an icon it is best that it should be at about eye level. The Orthodox usually stand before their icons, but that is a matter of choice, and less important than that we follow the rules for posture as earlier described. Distance must be judged according to what is comfortable in relation to the size of the icon.

There is a meditative use of icons and this we shall first describe. Taking up our position we look with a steady gaze, or it may be better to see the icon as looking at oneself. Our imagination is now allowed to play over the scene as it may over a scriptural passage in the ordinary way of meditative prayer. In either case we may 'intellectualize' so that the icon or the passage read may yield one or more devotional or theological points. Thus in my icon of the resurrection, Christ in raising Adam from the tomb is holding him by the wrist and not, as one might expect, grasping him by the hand, thus symbolizing that our salvation is all of God's doing. This is but one of a number of theological points which include the glory of the risen Christ, the triumph over the powers of darkness and so on. Often the icon may be a better medium than the written word for conveying truth. Thus Basil Minchin writes of the Rublev icon of the Trinity—'which many think is the greatest icon ever painted'—that to gaze upon the three figures sitting in 'restful dignity', their bodies forming a circle symbolizing unity, 'is a far better way to teach what the doctrine of the Trinity is all about than to recite the intellectualised cross-word puzzle which we call the Athanasian creed'. After we have looked upon the icon for a period we may move briefly into a simple way of affective prayer, and our vigil is thus brought to its close.

Many, however, will want to move on from the meditative form to discover through the medium of the icon a way of prayer which corresponds with the contemplative way described in the preceding chapters. Our introduction to this step may be made through an experiment in the secular field, which is suggestive of what we may experience at a deeper level in the use of icons. The psycho-physical content will be the same in each case, and it is at the spiritual level that the difference between the two must be sought.

In his book *The Natural History of the Mind* G. R. Taylor

speaks of an experiment made in America in which students were asked to sit in a quiet room and contemplate passively a small blue vase (about ten inches high) standing on a red-brown table. The subjects were instructed to let the perception of the vase fill the entire mind. Five minutes were allowed for the first day, ten minutes for the second, and then fifteen minutes; or the period could be prolonged if desired. Sometimes soft music was played; at other times there was complete silence.

What did these students find? All of them found that the colour of the vase became more intense, 'almost luminous'.

The outlines seemed to shift and dissolve. Most subjects felt that less time had elapsed than was usually the case. They became increasingly able to keep out distracting stimuli. More unexpectedly they became very attached to the vase and were disturbed if it was removed. As one subject said, 'I was nostalgic . . . it was like saying goodbye to a teacher of a course you had learnt something in, and had become involved in it and were sorry to leave it . . . the most vivid thing in the room.' All enjoyed the sessions.[6]

The vase became 'almost luminous' and its outline seemed to shift and dissolve'. It could be interesting to note a similarity here between the experience of the students and that of Julian before the crucifix at the time of her 'shewings'. As in the field of icons—where something similar may be experienced—this would be a fair comparison at the psycho-physical level. We have to remember, however, that this is not the only level nor is it the most important. Such resemblances, while of interest to the scientific observer, do not in fact take us very far. They tell us nothing of the essential nature of the activity of which the value must be judged by the intention.

Speaking still at the superficial level of body and mind we may go yet further and say that the vase experience on the one hand, and the icon or prayer experience on the other, would again be alike in that the brainwave pattern (as could be shown by the appropriate instruments) would undergo a change from the normal beta rhythm of ordinary life to that of alpha.[7] But this, too, would be nothing to do with prayer *as such* but with the relaxation which may be expected to accompany prayer, a relaxation which would also have been experienced by the students before the vase. Once more we have a physical accompaniment—this time relaxation—which taken simply in itself is morally neutral. We have as always to return to the area of intention which we have seen to be basic to the whole question of prayer. It is not anything which takes place at the level of the body, but the intention or the end pursued which is ultimately significant. The following passage written on contemplative prayer in relation to transcendental meditation has bearing here:

> Any relaxing experience such as Autogenic Training, contemplating an icon, holding a word or sentence in the heart, working in the kitchen as Brother Lawrence experienced it, knitting as many experience it, saying or chanting an office, can be a moving into alpha brainwave activity which brings with it new energies and a tranquil frame of mind. The Christian assesses their worth on whether they are to be found in the way of vocation, and engaged upon with God as their end. Whom seek ye? as always, is the vital question. Though I make alpha waves all the day long and have not charity I am nothing. Or as Aelred of Rievaulx has put it, 'Keep charity and nothing will be wanting you. Lose it and nothing will profit you.'[8]

We have said earlier that to the Orthodox Christian the icon is seen as a powerful channel of divine grace. This may be a difficult saying for some brought up in other traditions, but I think we may well know something not too unlike it in our own experience. I occasionally visit the Shrine of our Lady at Walsingham, and no visit is complete without a period in the chapel known as the Holy House at the centre of the Shrine. Hundreds of intercession requests are here displayed, and whenever one enters that place it seems as if the walls are dripping with prayer. It is an experience common to many, and many others who have never visited the Shrine can speak of similar if less intense experiences, usually in places long associated with prayer. If prayers can almost in a physical sense be seen as clinging to the walls of a building, it is no great extension of thought to see the same in relation to an icon. I recall being taken to the icon corner of a house and remarking later to my hosts that it had a charged atmosphere of its own. I was perhaps a little bit deflated when my observation was taken as being as banal as if I had said it was warmer near the fire. These good people simply took it for granted that it must be so. I do not think this 'spiritual charge' takes place simply through the blessing of an icon, but rather that it is built up through the constant prayers of the faithful. And I myself, together with most people, I imagine, would value an icon which had been soaked in prayer through the ages more than one taken clean and fresh out of the shop window. In the Orthodox Church this numinous quality associated with icons, and especially those hallowed by antiquity and closely linked with the saints, leads to their being taken to the sick as instruments of healing, much as handkerchiefs and clothing taken from St Paul were used in biblical times for this purpose.[9]

If now we look back to the experiment earlier described we shall see that the students were asked to contemplate the vase passively. The instruction might equally have been to sit before it in relaxed awareness, and this alternative way of expression may supplement the other in helping us to see what is required as we sit or stand before an icon. They were also told to let the perception of the vase fill the whole mind, and this too must be taken over into our vigil. There must not be room for anything to occupy the mind excepting the icon before us. Moreover the temptation must be resisted to indulge in deliberate theological speculation on the subject of the icon, for however good and desirable that may be at another time, this is not the place for it now. We may, however, allow the imagination to play gently over the icon if it will, but we are not to encourage it to do so. Distractions from outside sources will inevitably find their way in; we are to meet these by re-establishing our relationship with the icon, following the rules governing involuntary distraction set out in the previous chapter.

A time may come during the prayer period when it is best to close the eyes, putting the image of the icon in the heart, and from there allowing it to slip away as it will. If, however, we are at once left in an imageless stillness we need look for nothing more. One way or the other the icon becomes God's instrument by which he may establish his presence in the heart.

To pray before an icon can be of special help when the mind is tense or occupied with a miscellany of thoughts or ideas which the business of the day has brought upon us. We should, however, note that we ought never to try to force anything to happen. Whatever takes place should simply be allowed to do so in its own time. Our part is to look steadily—though unstrainedly—allowing the Holy Spirit to quicken our hearts and minds as and when he will.

*

What we have written on icons finds a natural extension to all our senses any of which may be used by God as partners in the life of prayer. For some the way in to contemplative silence may be found better through music than through visual aids. The same principles apply as those we have described. Naturally we choose our music with care and need to discover what will help us best. The listening is to be done in passive concentration, and the perception of the music and nothing else is to fill the entire mind. The music may 'play on' in the mind after the tape or record is ended. Finally it will disappear as we remain in stillness before God—'silent music', to use an expressive phrase of St John of the Cross.

The hearing of an office sung or chanted in a cathedral or monastic house can too be a great stimulus to the prayer of silence. People sometimes complain of a cathedral service that they are not expected to take part, but of course the truth is that we are being invited to participate in what may be the deepest way of all, the way of silence. There is room for experiment here in convents and monasteries, allowing groups in turn to sit apart so that they may silently assist the Office. Unfortunately this is sometimes seen as an opting out, but anyone who seriously attempts to participate in this way may well think that the choir has the easier part. One way is to transfer one's full awareness from one side of the choir to the other as each chants its appointed verse. It may, however, be better, and especially as the prayer life becomes more passive, simply to sit in relaxed awareness allowing the Office to sweep over one and enfold one, much as one may listen to a musical symphony. The holding of the posture is in itself an invaluable help in maintaining the true spirit of prayer.

So far I have never experimented with a group in the realm of taste or smell in the way outlined for sight and hearing. There is no difference in principle. There is no reason why a perfume—a flower perhaps—should not be smelt, or a wine sipped as a meditational aid. To take a liqueur chocolate—if we have one!—and to savour it slowly, putting one's full awareness into what one is doing, so that the perception of this and nothing else fills the mind, and to do this or something similar from time to time, is not simply a meditative experience, but a valuable corrective to the ordinary way in which we eat our food. I recall the emphasis placed on eating at the Zen Buddhist retreat. Tea-drinking was a contemplative exercise, and instead of music or a book at meals we had to put all our awareness into what we were doing, whether in the eating of our food or in the serving of one another. It is, we shall agree, but one way of eating a meal. We may serve one another by conversation, as, too, by passing the dishes; and if we are alone our awareness can be directed into channels other than our eating. Where it is directed is in fact secondary, what is primary being that we do not just moon.

Lastly there is the sense of touch. We may be grateful for advances made in our understanding here. Doctors and research workers are discovering that to deprive children of being touched is to threaten their emotional stability. The importance of breast-feeding, for a while out of fashion, is impressed on mothers today. Massage or merely stroking the skin are valued as having a relaxing effect on mind and body. Lack of tactile stimulation has been shown to have an important bearing on schizophrenia. Experiments with married couples who are drifting apart have shown that learning 'the very simplest non-sexual kind of touching' may be potent in bringing them together again. Simply to massage one another's feet is to activate nerve endings which reach into almost every part of the body.[10]

Yet how fearful we often are, and not least in our churches! I recall attending the Sung Eucharist in a West Country cathedral on Christmas Day. The bishop presided and gave us the sign of peace. Being a stranger I waited for the congregation to take it up, but no one stirred. I took the hands of the lady next to me and wished her Christ's peace. This would surely set things going; yet still no one moved. After the service, however, my neighbour asked me if I was a visitor, and, on learning that I was, invited me to share with the family in their Christmas lunch. It is a very simple parable. So much from so little! People are, I think, generally glad when in the way of friendliness someone else takes the initiative, and perhaps, fearing we shall be regarded as intruders and not as guests, we too often yield to a timidity in taking it ourselves. Yet, on the other hand, as Julian never ceases to remind us, God is supremely courteous, and a cordiality which would thrust itself unwillingly on another has no share in the divine charity. Even so, he who gives in good measure generally receives in return, and the giving and receiving of the peace with a few simple words can do much for a congregation. It is not just a matter of deepening fellowship and overcoming isolation, but in the first place a sign and quickener of the corporate nature of our worship and a reminder that the Body of Christ needs every member for its completion.

How different was the climate in the beginnings of the faith! Jesus is unembarrassed when a prostitute uses her fallen hair to wipe his feet. Paul bids Christians greet one another in friendly embrace. Jesus washes the feet of his disciples at the last supper and bids them serve one another as he has served them. Later the beloved disciple lies with his head reclining on Jesus' breast. How some of our modern translations wriggle here! Physical contact may mediate God's love more effectively than words can ever do. I recall how when I slipped a disc a friend from the church would come to my bedside and stroke my arms for twenty minutes. I had almost said her ministrations did me more good than prayer. But that would be a foolish way of putting it, for of course it *was* prayer.

Several years ago a mother would come to the Julian Cell almost every morning with her four-year-old son, and with her arms around him would pray in silence for half an hour. Sometimes he slept, sometimes he just stayed still, breaking away occasionally to wander round. We shall never know what that daily period meant. If it is a good thing to teach young children in some simple way to say their prayers, it is yet better—though the two naturally stand together—to hold and enfold them in the love of God; and this needs a physical as well as a spiritual dimension. So Jesus took young children into his arms as he blessed them.

But to return. It can be of great help to become aware of our bodies during prayer. In our Zen retreat we were instructed in meditative walking. Your awareness is to go into every step, and yet more into every movement which makes the step. This is a way of prayer, and it can be of enormous help when we are distracted and need to become centred. It can be adapted to walking in the street with no one knowing that anything special is taking place. Or when kneeling or sitting in prayer one may put one's awareness completely into a hand on the thigh, feeling its touch and warmth; or yet again into feeling the breath as it enters and leaves the nostrils, becoming aware of sensations quite unnoticed before. The possibilities can be extended beyond number. It all becomes prayer if the intention to pray is present. It is our offering, and it needs love and perseverance to carry it through.

Can we extend this matter of touch to others in formal prayer? Certainly, if we are of like mind and agreed that it will help. Probably it is best reserved for a short while towards the end of a period of prayer together. But we cannot rule for all, and there is plenty of room for exploration for husbands and wives, and others who have a warm and loving Christian friendship. It may be simply the clasping of the hand, or whatever more seems suitable. It is a carrying over of the love of God into the love of one another, a true loving of the other in God and for God.

*

And what are we to say of Julian in all this? Julian saw clearly that all our senses are in God's plan to be used in bringing us closer to him. Seeing and hearing, smelling and tasting and touching are one and all to be the instruments of our growth to wholeness and completeness in Christ. The fact that we often put our senses to trivial and destructive use makes it the more important that we stress that it is not only the spiritual part of ourselves, but our whole sensual nature which is the sphere of God's redeeming activity. Julian's special relevance to our age is in large measure to be found at this point. God's work is to restore our human nature, to lift it all up to himself, not to crush it to release some supposed spiritual essence as a man may crush grapes to extract the juice. It is not at all like this for, says Julian, 'I saw very surely that our substance is in God, and I also saw that God is in our sensuality, for in the same instant and place in which our soul is made sensual, in that same instant and place exists the city of God.'[11] In the following chapter Julian tells us that we can never be made holy until our sensuality is raised to the level of our substance.

There is a school of Christianity which appears to want to make man into an angel. The uninstructed reader of the lives of some of the desert fathers, for example, might be forgiven if he thought that that was what Christianity was about. Thus, in an account I have been reading recently, the fathers are described as living the angelic life, and later as looking like a real army of angels. Such expressions may be taken as figures of speech intended to convey the deep holiness of these men. The writer of the Acts of the Apostles uses similar words in describing Stephen before the Sanhedrin.[12] But when at another point we read of a father who has attained the angelic state, then—unless language is being used extremely loosely— we are in the presence of serious theological error. The sugges- tion is that the human nature which God has given us is just not good enough, and so we must get rid of it as quickly as we can, asking God to change it for something better. We are, of course, quoting the words of a reporter, and there is no need to assume that the fathers shared his blunder. The point is made to present a contrast with Julian. If someone had told Julian she was an angel, she would have protested strongly and clearly that she was a woman and that that was how God intended her to stay. She would probably too have taken her visitor in hand and given a homely instruction in incarnational theology. She would have explained that God in Jesus became man taking upon himself the fullness of our human nature in one who spoke and worked and lived as a man among men. Julian, as we have seen, is insistent that

God's concern reaches to every part of our human nature, and in a passage of exquisite delicacy which we have quoted in Chapter six she traces his handiwork right down to our humblest human needs. 'Our substance', she writes—meaning by this our essential nature—can rightly be called our soul, and 'our sensuality' too 'can rightly be called our soul, and that is by the union which it has in God'.[13] We cannot doubt that Julian would have told those whom she counselled that their senses in the design of God were to be the instruments through which their sanctification might be completed. Naturally, as frail men and women still on the way, we have to bring a watchful eye to the things of sense. We are as horses not yet fully broken in, which may snatch the bit between the teeth and bolt at any moment. Hence the Church in its wisdom provides fasting and abstinence—words which do not apply to food alone—but not, as we have seen, because the body is evil, but because, being good, it is to become a yet fitter instrument of the Holy Spirit.

All Shall be Well

'All Shall be Well and All Shall be Well and All Manner of Thing Shall be Well.' These are probably the only words—if any at all—which most people know as coming from the writings of Julian of Norwich. Many of us may use them from time to time, though perhaps not always wisely, for there is a danger lest they fall too easily—even glibly—from our lips. Uprooted from their context, they can be used as the expression of a sunny optimism, whereas Julian intended them as an assurance of the ultimate victory of love. They were born of much travail, their gestation period being one of physical suffering, temptation and spiritual anguish. We can use them safely only if we can make them our own, not just in the serene and happy periods of life, but when the foundations are shaken—in times of pain, doubt, depression, darkness and fear, which perhaps we know only too well.

When Julian wrote these words she was wrestling with the problem of sin as she saw it in herself and throughout the world. If only—as ever, vain thought, and Julian recognized it as such—sin had not been, then 'we should all have been pure and as like our Lord as he created us'.[1] So 'I mourned and sorrowed on this account, unreasonably, lacking discretion', and the Shorter Text adds, 'filled with pride'.[2] But the immortal words were given her: 'Sin is necessary, but all shall be well, and all shall be well, and all manner of thing shall be well.'[3] Many see this as Julian's deepest insight; others as her great heresy. How did she herself receive it? It seems from the Shorter Text written, we must remember, almost twenty years before the full text, and shortly after the revelations themselves, that what she had been given came as a considerable shock. At that point she did not reveal all that she had been told. Content with being about to reveal that 'sin is necessary',[4] and perhaps appalled that she will say so much, she throws herself into the arms of 'Holy Church', 'hungry and thirsty and needy and sinful and frail', willingly submitting herself with all her fellow-Christians to 'the teaching of Holy Church to the end of my life'.

How are we to understand the words, 'sin is behovabil', as Julian wrote, variously translated as 'necessary', 'inevitable', or 'sin must needs be'? We must begin with a word of caution. It is clearly unfair to any writer to fasten one's attention on some striking saying and attempt to interpret it without reference to the work as a whole. In Julian's case it happens that we are warned against this, not it is true by Julian herself, but by the scribe who may have written down her words, or perhaps later by some scribe editor. As a post-script to her work, this unknown writer says to her readers:

> I pray God Almighty that this book shall fall only into the hands of those who intend to be his lovers, and who are willing to submit to the Faith of Holy Church. . . . For this revelation contains deep theology and great wisdom, and is not meant for those who are enslaved by sin and the Devil. Beware of selecting only what you like, and leaving the rest. . . . Take it whole (and) all together.[5]

As we have seen, in spite of Julian's startling revelation, she does not deny the teaching of the Church, and it is made amply clear in the Longer Text that she accepts the Church's teaching on judgement and the last things. But I think that we may note that Julian is very much more specific on the teaching of the Church in the Longer Text than in the Shorter. It would be fascinating to know what lies behind the additions in the longer manuscript, whether Julian wrote them on her own initiative, or in response to representations made to her by—it may be—ecclesiastical authority, fearful lest her startling words, standing on their own, might be misrepresented or misunderstood.

How can we resolve the apparent contradiction to which our inquiry has taken us? The answer is that we cannot; we have to hold to both elements, drawing now on one, now on the other according to our needs. Once again we are caught up in the paradox between God's foreknowledge and man's free will. As I look back on my life with its sins and failures I can say with some confidence that they were necessary, that without them God could not have broken through the hard shell of pride which resisted mercy and grace. I needed my sins, not for their sake, but for the sake of the self-knowledge in which I must be grounded if the work of grace is to be made complete. I need them for the better understanding of the depth of the love which receives me again, and will never cast me off. So I see that my sins were necessary, and although as actions they are frozen hard in history, in value they for ever remain fluid to become the instrument of a deeper penitence and love. But they have, too, damaged others, and what then can I say? I must believe that they were foreseen and permitted from the beginning of time, and I must hand over their consequences to the mercy and wisdom of God, who can yet bring good out of evil and use suffering for the ultimate purpose of love. I have no right to expect that those whom I have hurt can share Julian's exalted insight that my sin was necessary, but in so far as it is given them to do so their forgiveness will contain within it an element of humble gladness that they have been chosen by God as instruments of my redemption. Thus may we all—may I add in parenthesis—by sharing in Christ's vicarious suffering become the agents of one another's healing.[6] 'This is (our) way of helping to complete in (our) poor human flesh, the full tale of Christ's afflictions still to be endured, for the sake of his body which is the Church.'[7]

So be it as I look back. Yet when I look forward I need to put those thoughts away, and I see myself responsible for what I do, exercising the gift of free will God has given me, my life open to the possibility of judgement and death. Time will come when what is now future will be gathered into the past, and then I shall look back and see that these sins too were necessary if the stubbornness which remains is to be broken through.

What I have written for myself, is it not the journey of everyman? Take the strange circumstances of Peter and his denial of his Lord. Did he never reflect that Jesus did not pray that it should not happen, but simply that after it had happened he might be a strength to the others?[8] Did not that in itself suggest that his sin was necessary, and foreseen as such by him who knew the hearts of all men? Peter's descent into the valley of humiliation, broken to be remade, humbled to be restored, purged to be cleansed, is a part of the odyssey of every Christian soul. We can never fathom the bleakness of those few days verging on despair, unrelieved by hope that he would ever see his friend again. Peter, too, suffered death and resurrection as presumption and self-confidence gave way to humility and faith. Peter never spares himself in the telling of his fall, but the record is factual with no trace of bitterness or recrimination. We may believe that he had come not merely to accept it, but to see that it was necessary, that he might see himself in the light of reality rather than in that of his own fancy.

It seems to me that thoughts such as these do justice to both sides of Julian's writing. On the one hand we have this deeply evocative passage from chapter 61:

And then he allows some of us to fall more severely and painfully than ever before—or so it seems to us. And then we (not all of whom are wise), think it was a waste of time to have started at all. It is not so, of course. We need to fall, and we need to realise this. If we never fell we should never know how weak and wretched we are in ourselves; nor should we fully appreciate the astonishing love of our Maker. In heaven we shall really and eternally see that we sinned grievously in this life: yet despite all this, we shall also see that it made no difference at all to his love, and we were no less precious in his sight. By the simple fact that we fell we shall gain a simple and wonderful knowledge of what God's love means. Love that cannot, will not, be broken by sin, is rock-like, and quite astonishing. It is a good thing to know this. Another benefit is the sense of insignificance and humbling that we get by seeing ourselves fall. Through it, as we know, we shall be raised up to heaven: but such exaltation might never have been ours without the prior humbling. We have *got* to see this. If we do not, no fall would do us any good. Normally we fall first, and see afterwards—and both through God's mercy.[9]

That on the one hand as we look backwards, and then on the other as we look ahead:

> But if, because of all this spiritual comfort we have been talking of, one were foolish enough to say, 'If this is true, it is a good thing to sin because the reward will be greater', or to hold sin less sinful, then beware! Should such a thought come it would be untrue, and would stem from the enemy of the very love that tells of all this comfort. The same blessed love tells us that we should hate sin for Love's sake alone. I am quite clear about this.'. . . The soul by its very nature can have no hell but sin. . . . We are to hate sin absolutely, we are to love the soul eternally, just as God loves it. Our hatred of sin will be like God's hatred of it; our love of the soul like God's.[10]

Julian's writings abound in contrast, but always it is that the work of mercy and grace is uppermost: 'He taught me that I should contemplate the glorious atonement, for this atoning is more pleasing to the blessed divinity and more honourable for man's salvation, without comparison, than ever Adam's sin was harmful.'[11]

Where sin is followed by repentance the problem is relieved. Julian cites the example of St John of Beverley as standing for many others:

> St John of Beverley our Lord showed vividly, a comfort to us because he was so homely and unaffected . . . in his young and tender years . . . a very dear servant of God, loving and fearing God very greatly. Yet God allowed him to fall, though in his mercy he kept him from perishing, and from losing ground. Afterwards God raised him to much greater grace, and because of the humility and contrition of his life, in heaven God has given him many joys, greater even than those he would have had had he never fallen.[12]

It is where repentance does not follow sin that great mystery remains. Julian never penetrated that mystery. She speaks of a great deed to be done at the end of time, but it takes her in no way forward in her understanding: 'What the deed will be and how it will be performed is unknown to every creature.'[13] God's word to Julian was that she must wait in faith and trust; only at the end of all things would she be able to see. 'Accept it now in faith and trust, and in the very end you will see truly, in fullness of joy.'

Julian's great love for her fellow-men meant that the problem of sin pressed upon her with great urgency. Not only is she puzzled, but she is in anguish and turmoil as she looks around the world and sees the ravages of sin, and the pain it brings to God's creation. She calls out: 'Lord, how can everything be well when such pain has come to your creatures through sin?'[14] There are so many deeds, she writes, that are so wicked that it seems impossible for us to believe that any good will come of them. And she adds that in dwelling upon these things—and it seems that at times she felt she must do so—it is impossible to rest in the contemplation of God as we ought to do. Later she received the assurance that what is impossible for us is not impossible for God, who would honour his word in every respect and indeed make all things well.[15] Like ourselves she was never able to understand, but she was taught that it was unprofitable to allow her anxiety and misgivings to take her away from the contemplation of God. This is an important lesson, and the work of prayer must be undermined in the failure to learn it.

It can very well be with us, as with Julian, that some secondary matter holds our attention, and takes us away from our primary task of waiting on God. In Julian's case the issue was the problem of evil, and she was taught to see the vanity of her pursuit. She writes that it was a line of thought which ought to have been left well alone, though 'as it was I grieved and sorrowed over it, with neither cause nor justification'[16]; and a little later[17] she says rather quaintly that God has a right to be left undisturbed in his own business, and it was not for her to try to pry into his secrets.

It is beside the point that we are not big enough people to have such unselfish concerns as Julian's. Our liberty is equally curtailed whether we are bound by rough hemp or a silken cord. Any anxiety or problem, any curiosity or pursuit, may so take hold of us as to make for the undermining of the prayer life. These may belong to the area of the obviously destructive, such as self-pity, immoderate self-accusation or fears moving on to despair; but equally, and perhaps more insidiously, occupations good and right in themselves may become the enemy of the best. So long as the worship of God is given its rightful priority, then the rest will fall into place and may be seen as the overspill of prayer into daily life. Lesser things pursued as ends can never satisfy, and make for restlessness and disquiet. It seems that this was the experience of Julian as she discovers that to 'sorrow and mourn' over the mysteries beyond our ken takes us away from 'the blessed contemplation of God as we ought to do'.[18] In him alone are we to find our peace, a thought she has expressed earlier in words of haunting beauty:

> This is the cause why we are not at rest in heart and soul; that here we seek rest in things that are so little there is no rest in them, and we do not know our God who is all mighty, all wise and all good. For he is true rest. No soul can have rest until it finds created things are empty. When the soul gives up all for love, so that it can have him that is all then it finds true rest. . . . For he is endless and has made us for his own self only, and has restored us by his blessed Passion, and keeps us in his blessed love. And he does all this through his goodness. . . . God of your goodness give me yourself, for you are enough for me.[19]

When Julian uttered her famous words, 'All shall be well', she did not, of course, mean that in the short run everything will be well in the sense that we shall be spared suffering, sorrow, doubt, poverty and anxiety and all the other pains which assault men and women everywhere. If her words are true here and now, it is in the important sense that God's grace can be counted upon to deliver us *through* trial and not necessarily *from* it. God's deliverance from trial may not be his highest compliment, but rather a concession to our immaturity and lack of faith.

A story from the gospel bears eloquent witness to this. The disciples are caught in a raging storm on the Sea of Galilee.[20] We are presented with the contrast between these badly frightened men toiling at the oars, and Jesus asleep on a cushion in the stern of the boat. Panic-stricken, they arouse him, and Jesus, we are told, rebukes the wind and the waves and there is a great calm. But it is not only the storm which was rebuked. Jesus then turned to these men and rebuked them for their lack of faith. It would have been better if they could have passed through the storm as he himself was prepared to do. Their deliverance can be seen as a concession to their faithlessness and their weakness. The story stands as a parable of our life situations—the troubles, distresses, anxieties we meet with in the way. Julian uses much the same imagery in one of her most famous passages:

He did not say, 'You shall not be tempest-tossed, you shall not be work-weary, you shall not be discomforted'. But he said, 'You shall not be overcome.' God wants us to heed these words so that we shall always be strong in trust, both in sorrow and in joy.[21]

Julian's own words near the end of her book are perhaps the finest commentary on her great saying:

When judgement is given and we are all brought up above, then we shall see clearly in God the secrets now hidden from us. In that day not one of us will want to say, 'Lord, if it had been done this way, it would have been well done'. But we shall all say with one voice, 'Lord, blessed may you be. For it is so, and it is well. And now we see truly that all things are done as it was ordained before anything was made'.[22]

Notes

CHAPTER 1. *Julian and Her Cell Today*

1. Thomas Merton's tribute is taken from an article in *Mount Carmel*, Winter 1977, by Hilary Costello, ocso, who thought the letter might then have been unpublished, and perhaps is so still. The full quotation from Thomas Merton reads:

   > Julian is without doubt one of the most wonderful of all Christian voices. She gets greater and greater in my eyes as I grow older, and whereas in the old days I used to be crazy about St John of the Cross, I would not exchange him now for Julian if you gave me the world and the Indies and all the Spanish mystics rolled up in one bundle. I think that Julian of Norwich is with Newman the greatest English theologian.

2. T. W. Coleman, *English Mystics of the Fourteenth Century* (Epworth Press 1938), p. 131.
3. F. Blomefield, *History of the County of Norfolk* (London 1806), vol. iv, p. 81.
4. St Julian's Church, Norwich, situated in St Julian's Alley, which links Rouen Road with King Street. The church lies about half a mile south of Norwich Cathedral.
5. *The Book of Margery Kempe*, ed. Meech and Lane (Oxford University Press 1961); published for the Early English Text Society, vol. i, p. 42, lines 18–20.
6. The Longer Text will be referred to throughout the notes as LT; the Shorter Text as ST.
7. LT 3, *Revelations of Divine Love*, tr. Clifton Wolters (Penguin Classics 1973). This translation is referred to throughout as CW. See also ST 2.
8. LT 3, CW. See also ST 2.
9. LT 3, CW. See also ST 2. (See LT 66, CW for temporary return of sickness between the fifteenth and sixteenth showings. Not recorded in ST.)

10. ST 10, *Julian of Norwich: Showings,* tr. Edmund Colledge, OSA, and James Walsh, SJ. (SPCK 1979). This translation is referred to throughout as EC and JW.
11. LT 3, EC and JW.
12. A. M. Allchin, *The Dynamic of Tradition* (Darton, Longman and Todd 1981), p. 5.
13. LT 61.
14. A. M. Allchin, op. cit., p. 38. The full quotation from Thomas Merton reads:

> She is a true theologian with greater clarity, depth and order than St Teresa; she really elaborates, theologically, the content of her revelations. She first experienced, then thought, and the thoughtful deepening of experience worked itself back into her life, deeper and deeper, until her whole life as a recluse at Norwich was simply a matter of getting completely saturated in the light she had received all at once, in the 'shewings', when she thought she was about to die.

From *Conjectures of a Guilty Bystander* by Thomas Merton (New York, Doubleday, 1968), p. 191.
15. ST 6.
16. ST 6.

CHAPTER 2. Humility True and False

1. LT 73. *Enfolded in Love* (Darton, Longman and Todd 1980), p. 46. This book will be referred to throughout as E in L.
2. LT 73, EC and JW.
3. LT 73, EC and JW. See also ST 24.
4. LT 73, E in L, p. 46. See also ST 24.
5. LT 10, EC and JW.
6. LT 75, EC and JW.
7. LT 7, E in L, p. 8.
8. LT 6, E in L, p. 8.
9. John 21:18.
10. 1 Cor. 3:2.
11. J.-P. de Caussade, SJ, *Self-Abandonment to Divine Providence,* tr. Algar Thorold (Burns and Oates 1959), Book VII, Letter 18.
12. D. Considine, SJ, *Words of Encouragement* (Catholic Truth Society 1978), Part 3, p. 6.
13. LT 28, CW.
14. LT 28, EC and JW.

15. LT 77, CW.
16. LT 77, E in L, p. 50.

CHAPTER 3. The Wrath is not in God

1. LT 49, E in L, p. 25.
2. LT 46, EC and JW.
3. LT 48, EC and JW.
4. 1 Cor.11:29.
5. LT 39, E in L, p. 17.
6. LT 76, E in L, p. 48.
7. Caroll E. Simcox, *A Treasury of Quotations on Christian Themes* (SPCK 1976), no. 139. Original source not traced.
8. LT 46, EC and JW.
9. Eph. 2:8–9.
10. LT 48, EC and JW.
11. LT 82, EC and JW.
12. LT 82, E in L, p. 55.
13. LT 48, EC and JW.
14. LT 50, EC and JW.
15. Rom. 7:24.
16. LT 51, E in L, pp. 27–8.
17. From a book of poems by Monica Furlong: *God's a Good Man and other Poems* (Mowbray 1974). It is perhaps worth commenting that while man can never be more generous than God, he may be—and mercifully often is—more generous than his conscious conception of God.
18. LT 73, E in L, p. 46.
19. LT 79, E in L, p. 52.
20. LT 77, E in L, p. 49.
21. LT 59, E in L, p. 35.
22. LT 60, E in L, p. 36.
23. LT 61, E in L, p. 37.
24. LT 61, E in L, p. 38.

CHAPTER 4. Falling We Stand

1. LT 82, E in L, p. 53.
2. I am indebted to Michael McLean, *The Perfectest Herald of Joy*. Julian Shrine Publication.

3. The reference is to Gal. 2:11ff.
4. See Acts 10 and 15:1–29 for the heart of the issue before the early Church.
5. 1 Cor. 11:3–16.
6. John 18:37.
7. D. Bonhoeffer, *Ethics* (SCM Press 1978), pp. 330–1.
8. Thus a deeper truth is served in protecting a confidence than in satisfying an idle curiosity, and this may involve an 'untruth', a denial, perhaps, of one's knowledge in the matter raised. It is clear that in such a case truth to one's questioner would in fact be untruth to the one to whom secrecy had been promised.
9. The point is well made in a charge given in 1931 by William Temple to the clergy of the Province of York. He was speaking on the practice of receiving Holy Communion in a period when the fast from midnight was general. The early morning celebration was customary, and evening communion would have been regarded widely as impossible or at least as a more than dubious innovation. A précis of what the Archbishop said might run like this:

> To make the reception of Holy Communion the first nourishment of the day may be most properly commended as a manifestation and quickener of reverence and as an expression of fellowship with the greater part of the Church. But to make a binding rule on such a point and to say, as some have done, that to receive Holy Communion after breaking fast is a mortal sin—which by definition separates from God—must be pronounced idolatrous, for it involves a conception of God incompatible with the revelation of Jesus Christ.

> It would not, however, have been without anxiety and cost to many to put on their freedom in Christ in this area of the Christian life.

CHAPTER 5. Two Hindrances to Freedom

1. LT 52, CW.
2. Martin Thornton, 'The Cultural Factor in Spirituality', in Christopher Martin (ed.) *The Great Christian Centuries to Come* (Mowbray 1974), p. 183.
3. See Karlfried Von-Durkheim, *Hara, The Vital Centre of Man*, tr. Sylvia-Monica Von Kospoth (Allen and Unwin 1962), pp. 90ff.
4. Lest this sentence be misunderstood, let me affirm my belief

that there will always be some called to total abstention either as a personal discipline, or as an encouragement to others, or as a witness against the evils of alcoholic excess. However to turn what may be a precept for some into a rule for all would seem to involve the Church in a denial of the goodness of one part of God's creation. And so far as witness goes, the example of responsible drinking in a society given to excess is, too, a testimony in its own way. The argument in the text is, of course, not on the merits of partaking or abstaining, but on the exercising of our freedom in Christ, which may be expressed whichever course we pursue.

5. See David Cox, *Analytical Pyschology: An Introduction to the Work of C. G. Jung.* Hodder and Stoughton 1973. Chapter 7 on Psychic Development, to which I am gratefully indebted, develops the psychology underlying our theme. To the appearance of evil Cox adds the appearance of triviality and foolishness. (p. 137).

CHAPTER 6. Human Nature Restored

1. The full collect as used at St Julian's Church reads:

    Most Holy Lord, the ground of our beseeching, who through your servant Julian revealed the wonder of your love: grant that as we are created in your nature and restored by your grace, our wills may be so made one with yours, that we may come to see you face to face and gaze on you for ever, through. . . .

2. LT 55, EC and JW.
3. P. F. Chambers, *Julian of Norwich* (Gollancz 1955), pp. 19–20.
4. LT 63, EC and JW.
5. LT 6, EC and JW. Found in Paris MS. only.
6. Paul Verghese, *The Freedom of Man*, quoted in Kenneth Leech, *The Social God* (Sheldon Press 1981).
7. Luke 7:44–6.
8. Matthew 11:19.
9. 1 John 1:1.
10. 1 Tim. 4:4. The fruit of the Spirit, temperance (moderation) or self-control (Gal. 5:23), is naturally assumed throughout.
11. St John of the Cross, *Ascent of Mount Carmel,* Book III, chapter 24.
12. LT 43, E in L, p. 24.

13. John Robinson, *The Roots of a Radical* (SCM Press 1980), p. 149.
14. LT 58, E in L, p. 35.
15. June Singer, *Boundaries of the Soul* (Gollancz 1972), p. 140.
16. J. A. Hadfield, *Psychology and Morals* (Methuen 1937), p. 166. The whole passage is instructive.

CHAPTER 7. *Julian and Prayer: Yearning*

1. LT 46, EC and JW.
2. LT 72, EC and JW.
3. LT 81, EC and JW.
4. LT 42, EC and JW.
5. LT 41, EC and JW.
6. LT 46, EC and JW.
7. LT 72, EC and JW.
8. LT 43, EC and JW.
9. LT 82, EC and JW.
10. LT 31, EC and JW.
11. *The Nun's Rule Being The Ancren Riwle Modernised By James Morton* (Alexander Moring 1905), p. 37.
12. LT 70, ST 23, EC and JW.
13. *The Nun's Rule*, p. 13.
14. Evelyn Underhill, *Worship* (Nisbet 1936), p. 27.
15. Shirley Hughson, OHC, *Contemplative Prayer* (Holy Cross Press 1955), pp. 184–5.

CHAPTER 8. *Julian and Prayer: Beseeching*

1. LT 41, 42, 43. See also ST 19, EC and JW.
2. ST 19, EC and JW.
3. LT 2, EC and JW.
4. LT 2, ST 1, EC and JW.
5. LT 2, ST 1, EC and JW.
6. LT 41, EC and JW.
7. ST 19, EC and JW.
8. LT 41, ST 19, EC and JW.
9. ST 19, EC and JW.
10. R. M. Benson, SSJE, *Look to the Glory* (Canada, Society of Saint John the Evangelist 1966), p. 103.
11. ST 19, EC and JW.

12. LT 41, EC and JW.
13. ST 19, EC and JW.
14. LT 41, EC and JW.
15. LT 42, EC and JW.
16. Psalm 56:8.
17. LT 42, CW. There is an interesting resemblance here to St Teresa who in chapter 39 of her *Life* says she is only able to pray for the things God is going to do. Returning to Julian, prayer 'benefits us' because of its unitive aspect. Wherever prayer is real the deepening of our relationship with God must necessarily follow. Prayer 'oneth the soul to God', as Julian writes in her following chapter.
18. John 9:1–3.
19. Aelred Graham, *The Love of God* (Longmans 1939), p. 138.
20. Acts 12:5.
21. Ronald Knox, *The Pastoral Sermons* (Burns and Oates 1960).
22. The names and dates have been changed. In quoting this letter the writer has asked me to stress that it is only in the power of God's grace 'freely given to us' that she and her husband have been able to meet their situation.
23. 1 Thess. 5:18.
24. LT 6, CW.
25. E in L, p. 5. Taken from LT 6.

CHAPTER 9. Julian and Prayer: Beholding

1. LT 41, EC and JW.
2. LT 43. 'Oneth' belongs to the medieval text.
3. LT 43, EC and JW.
4. ST 19, EC and JW.
5. LT 41, 42, 43.
6. LT 43, EC and JW.
7. LT 43, EC and JW.
8. LT 14, E in L, p. 10.
9. Matthew 17:2, Mark 9:2.
10. 2 Cor. 12:2ff.
11. William Wordsworth's poem, 'I Wandered Lonely as a Cloud'.
12. LT 43, EC and JW.
13. *The Cloud of Unknowing and Other Works*, tr. Clifton Wolters (Penguin Classics 1978), ch. 26. Referred to throughout as CU, CW.
14. LT 8. See too ST 6, EC and JW. For 'Jesus has' I have

substituted 'if Jesus had' which, though not faithful to the original—a scribal error perhaps—seems to be clearly the meaning. So too CW.
15. LT 9. See too ST 6, EC and JW.
16. LT 41, EC and JW.
17. Robert Llewelyn, *Prayer and Contemplation*. (Oxford, SLG Press 1975). Slightly adapted.
18. Matthew 7:7, Luke 11:9.
19. The actual words 'acquired' and 'infused' (as distinct from what they denote) belong to two centuries and more after Julian's time.
20. LT 10, EC and JW.
21. CU 26. I have taken here the literal rendering of the Middle English.

CHAPTER 10. The Greatest Revelation is Stillness

1. Acts 17:34.
2. I am indebted to James Walsh, SJ. See p. 11 of his introduction to *The Revelations of Divine Love of Julian of Norwich*. Anthony Clarke 1973.
3. The figure of speech is from St Augustine.
4. CU 6, CW.
5. PC 3, CW.
6. LT 55, EC and JW.
7. Verrier Elwyn, *Richard Rolle*.
8. Written of Søren Kierkegaard. Source not traced.
9. CU 61, CW.
10. Brother Lawrence, *The Practice of the Presence of God*.
11. Ignatius of Loyola, *Spiritual Exercises*, First week. Section IV. It may be interesting to compare with Father Augustine Baker (author of *Holy Wisdom*) who in his *Confessions* (p. 105) says that his positions in prayer were as various as kneeling, sitting, walking and lying down, and that he ever accommodated his body to the state of his spirit.
12. Phil. 2:12–13.

CHAPTER 11. The Cloud of Unknowing

1. PC 5, CW.
2. PC 1, CW.

3. PC 2, CW.
4. CU 33, CW.
5. The reader is referred to CU, chapters 3, 5, 6, 7, 31, 32, 39. Based freely on CW.
6. CU 7, CW.
7. CU 8, CW.
8. CU 10, CW.
9. CU 31, CW.
10. CU 10, CW.
11. CU 33, CW.
12. CU 3, CW.
13. CU 32, CW.
14. CU 32, CW.
15. J.-P. de Caussade, SJ, *Self-Abandonment to Divine Providence,* tr. Algar Thorold (Burns and Oates 1959), Book v, Letter 15.
16. Compare with CU 41, CW. The writer explains that formal contemplation may be impossible in times of sickness, adding that it is the intention which matters. The chapter closes with the words:

    > So for the love of God control your body and soul alike with great care, and keep as fit as you can. Should illness come in spite of everything, have patience and wait humbly for God's mercy. That is all that is asked. For I tell the truth when I say that patience in sickness and other kinds of tribulation often pleases God far more than any pleasant devotion you might show in health.

CHAPTER 12. *Distractions are for Healing*

1. For those unfamiliar with a prayer stool, it can be described thus. The horizontal bridge may be about 16 inches long and 4 or 5 inches wide. Thickness a quarter to half an inch. A convenient height from the ground for most people is 7 inches. The supports to the bridge will be about 12 inches apart. You kneel down with legs under the bridge and between the supports, and then sit on the bridge, making an excellent support for the back. In case the reader has not got the idea, if the whole be turned upside-down it makes a book-rack.
2. Eph. 6:12.
3. William Johnston, SJ, *The Still Point.* (Fordham University Press 1980).

4. Robert Llewelyn, *The Positive Role of Distraction in Prayer*. Oxford, SLG Press 1977.

5. CU 33, CW.

6. Kallistos Ware, *The Power of the Name*. Oxford, SLG Press 1975.

7. St Teresa of Avila, *Interior Castle*. Fourth Mansion, ch I.

8. Michael McLean, *The Perfectest Herald of Joy*. (Julian Shrine Publication).

9. Maria Boulding, OSB, *Marked for Life*. (SPCK 1979).

10. It may, however, be noted that in a demonic situation Jesus ultimately uses the simple command 'Go' (Matt. 4:10). The familiar Authorised Version is, of course, 'Get thee hence'. It is interesting to compare this with *The Cloud* which commends the repeated use of the word 'out' in the repelling of evil. All the energies of the soul are to be gathered into the exercise. It needs to be stressed that this practice in no way involves the fastening of the mind or imagination on the evil but only on the command itself. 'Out' has become for the time being a more suitable word than 'God' or 'Love' which *The Cloud* also commends. The reader is referred to *The Cloud of Unknowing*, chapters 36–40. It should, however, be noted that in the Penguin Classics edition to which we have referred throughout, the word 'out' has been rendered 'help'.

CHAPTER 13. The Help of the Senses

1. LT 70, ST 23, EC and JW.

2. LT 3, CW. See also ST 2, EC and JW.

3. ST 21, EC and JW. LT 66 says 'in front of my face', but the two need not perhaps be contradictory.

4. St Basil the Great, quoted from Leonid Ouspensky, *Theology of the Icon* (New York, St Vladimir's Seminary Press, 1978), p. 10.

5. Basil Minchin, *Praying with Icons,* Julian Shrine Publication, to whom I am gratefully indebted in this paragraph.

6. G. R. Taylor, *The Natural History of the Mind*. Secker and Warburg 1979.

7. Those interested in this accompaniment of prayer may care to refer to ch. 3 (Brainwave and Biofeedback) of *Silent Music* by William Johnston, SJ (Collins 1974).

8. Robert Llewelyn, *Contemplative Prayer in Relation to Transcendental Meditation*. Julian Shrine Leaflet.

9. Acts 19:12. Work in the field of radionics appears to have bearing on what is written in the text. See *Radionics: Theory and*

Practice by John Wilcox, (Herbert Jenkins 1960), for two re-markable radionic photographs of water before and after bless-ing. A bright cross fills the picture of the second photograph. A portion of page 85 reads:

> It must always be borne in mind that whatever it is that is being photographed it is not the object itself, that is to say, not the physical or material aspect of it, which is all that is perceptible to the physical senses. Objects have residing in them or associated with them qualities and conditions apper-taining to their primary or fourth dimensional states, the pres-ence of which cannot be detected through the agency of the five senses.

Holy water, as is well known, is used in the exorcism of people or places, and it is not unreasonable to suppose that spirits can detect properties in it not perceptible to human beings (at least not ordinarily so) and respond accordingly. Work done in the field of psychometry is also suggestive here. See Leslie Weather-head, *Psychology, Religion and Healing*. (Hodder and Stoughton 1968), pp. 213ff. The reference is to the work of R. Connell, MD, FRCPI and Geraldine Cummins. The actual word 'psychom-etry' is not used.

10. George Downing, *The Massage Book* (Penguin 1974).

> In the sole of the foot are concentrated literally tens of thou-sands of nerve endings, and the opposite ends of these nerves are located all over the rest of the body. Thus the foot is a 'map' of the entire body. No muscle, no gland, no organ whether internal or external is without a set of nerves whose opposite ends are anchored in the foot (p. 93).

For some of the other information in this paragraph see book under note 6.

11. LT 55, EC and JW.
12. Acts 6:15.
13. LT 56, EC and JW.

CHAPTER 14. All Shall be Well

1. LT 27, ST 13, EC and JW.
2. ST 13, EC and JW.
3. LT 27.
4. ST 13, EC and JW.

5. Post-script to LT, CW.
6. The point is splendidly illustrated in the magnificent words of a Russian bishop as he went to his death in one of Stalin's purges: 'There will come a day when the martyr will be able to stand before the throne of God in defence of his persecutors and say, "Lord, I have forgiven in thy name and by thy example. Thou hast no claim against them any more." '
7. Col. 1:24.
8. Luke 22:31ff.
9. LT 61, CW.
10. LT 40, CW.
11. LT 29, ST 14, EC and JW.
12. LT 38, CW.
13. LT 32, EC and JW.
14. LT 29.
15. LT 32.
16. LT 27, CW.
17. LT 30.
18. LT 32, EC and JW.
19. LT 5, E in L, p. 4.
20. Mark 4:35ff.
21. LT 68, E in L, p. 39.
22. LT 85, E in L, p. 58.

p. 20